Zoran Stamenić

Belgrade's history
from the numismatic record

by

Adam Crnobrnja

Nikola Crnobrnja

BELGRADE CITY MUSEUM

Monographies 11

Published by:
Belgrade City Museum

Editor in chief:
Bojan Kovačević

Reviewed by:
Bojana Borić-Brešković

Translation:
Marina Adamović-Kulenović

Graphic design:
Zorica Spasojević /ALEXANDRIA STUDIO/

Photographs by:
Nebojša Borić, Vladimir Popović

Conservation expert:
Adam N. Crnobrnja

Circulation:
1200 copies

Print
ALEXANDRIA STUDIO

ISBN 86-80619-29-9

Preface to the English edition

Leafing through this book, the reader may mistake it for a mere catalogue of coins from the Belgrade City Museum collections, an overview of the pieces that have survived and were discovered, indeed rescued from the merciless passing of time. On closer examination, however, from the sum of all instants and epochs making up the last twenty-three centuries of historic time emerges the continuity of material culture on Belgrade's soil. The Coin and Medal Cabinet of the Belgrade City Museum possesses a collection that is very respectable both in width and in depth. Many periods, states and cultures in the political or monetary orbit of which Belgrade once was have their representatives in this book. In addition to a thorough look at Belgrade's long history, it has to offer several rare or unique pieces, such as the gold minimi of the Celtic tribe of Scordisci dating from the first century BC, or the first ever registered motif of the cross, on a coin of the Roman empress Salonina issued in AD 265.

A picture of the past drawn from vestiges of material culture may be consistent and legible enough, much like a puzzle never completed but nonetheless offering a recognizable shape, a reliable suggestion of the global scene. It feels good to hope that, by a stroke of fortune, some of the crucially important missing pieces of that puzzle will crop up. Not long before preparations for this book have started, the Belgrade City Museum came into possession of one of the six known gold coins of the Sultan Süleyman I minted at Belgrade in 1562–66.

Universal in every respect, specific in many respects and unique in some respects, money is a way of, and an avenue to, understanding history and culture. Throughout the ages these artefacts, physically small but symbolically and formally huge, form a cultural time continuum as hardly any or even no other field of human contrivance. The primeval jingle of coins or the soft rustle of paper notes in the hands of kings or farmers alike, their everyday presence and the ability to pass unharmed through time endow this human invention with a lasting academic and popular appeal.

Bojan Kovačević
Director of the Belgrade City Museum

Belgrade's history
from the numismatic record

Belgrade is the city with a long and eventful past. It belongs among the earliest cities in Europe, the thread of urban life running uninterrupted for more than two thousand years. The pages of its history have been written by many cultures, civilizations and state formations, and all of them left a trace behind: streets, buildings, cemeteries – we keep discovering them; relics of the material culture – we keep gathering and protecting them from complete ruin and oblivion. Money has also survived. In the past 160 years since the beginning of the more or less regular recording of archaeological finds from Belgrade and its environs, a wealth of old coins has been discovered. From one piece to another, the reader of this book will not only gain an insight into the two-millennium-long history of this city but also into the beauty of metallic and paper money circulating in the land between the Sava and Danube rivers over the centuries.

When about the year 700 BC in Lydia in Asia Minor a shaped piece of precious metal of guaranteed weight became a medium of exchange for goods and commodities for the first time, the pace of civilization gained speed. That invention, money – embraced and improved by the ancient Greeks and Romans – is but a fraction of the classical world's legacy that modern civilization rests on. In addition to this basic function and role – the equivalent of goods – that money had and still has, its properties defining it as a culture-historical document of its times should also be borne in mind. On money, written and artistically designed monuments, events are recorded, victories celebrated and ideas from the ruler's, religious or military spheres of life promoted. Money has retained those properties throughout history, as evidenced by modern issues. Thus money and its designs may be seen and interpreted from more than one aspect: as denominations with a certain market value, as historical documents, as art works (often of outstanding quality), as artefacts testifying to commercial links between regions, as a medium of propaganda. And yet, the common message conveyed by money ever since its invention, both through its iconography and by virtue of its being issued at a given moment, is statehood. From the very beginning of minting it is by issuing money that states have announced their existence and by a careful choice of designs that they have striven to demonstrate their distinctiveness, their policies and their strength.

For at least twenty-three centuries has money been present in the area of Belgrade. The first protagonists of a money economy on this soil were the Celts, i.e. the Scordisci, who established early contacts with the Hellenistic and then the Roman world. They struck their own coinage from the second century BC. Towards the end of the pre-Christian era the Danube Basin was conquered by the Romans. They built a series of forts along the river to protect and defend the state against barbarian incursions. It became possible for a town to grow at the side of a Roman military camp in present-day Kalemegdan, accommodating some 4–5 thousand well-paid legionary troops. The needs were diverse, and there flourished crafts, trade... Money began to flow, and it has been going on for centuries.

***

Fifty years ago the Belgrade City Museum founded a numismatic collection. Its founder, and the most praiseworthy for its growth, was Dr. Vladimir Kondić (1932–1994). The first pieces came from archaeological surveys and excavations undertaken after World War II. As the number of numismatic finds increased year by year, a department was founded assigned with accumulating money that had circulated in the Belgrade area for centuries. Set from the outset, high standards of selection have made the Collection very valuable. They are clear and simple: always make sure to note where the money is found, make checks and record the context and details of finds; maintain the associated documentation properly. In addition to the thousands of antique and medieval coins recovered, the discovery of several hoards has offered the possibility of studying a number of monetary phenomena such as money flows or the distribution of issues struck by different mints. Although it is not the traditional goal of coin collecting that has been pursued – to get hold of as rare, as beautiful, as well-preserved, as unusual piece as possible, the Collection is not short of unique pieces, or precious for the history of a currency. In the chapters that follow some of the pieces will be paid special attention.

In the early 1970s the Collection was enriched with two outstanding donations made by two exquisite connoisseurs and gifted coin collectors. Professor Svetozar St. Dušanić (1907–1990), years-long Director of the Museum of the Serbian Orthodox Church, donated to the city and its Museum his personal collection of Roman coins comprising the local issues of Stobi (Gradsko near Veles, Macedonia), Viminacium (near modern Kostolac) and the province of Dacia, a total of 2178 pieces. Each piece being furnished with information about its provenance, it is observable that many came from sites in the environs of Belgrade. Even after his donation became part of the Museum's collections, Prof. Dušanić continued to collect the coinage of those mints contributing to the legacy till the end of his life.

Quite outstanding is also the other gift – the collection of Djordje Novaković (1910–1968), a SFRY diplomat, which includes 7436 paper notes of the Kingdom of Serbia, of every Yugoslavia in existence during the legator's lifetime and a vast number of banknotes from virtually all European states. The paper money presented here comes from this legacy.

It would be unjust not to mention in this context that the Collection has been augmented individually as well. During the past fifty years, especially in the late 1950s and early 1960s, the villagers of Ritopek, Višnjica, Brestovik, Ušće and Skela used to bring coins to the Museum for sale and never failed to provide information about the location of their finds. Then reselling and "collecting" began to prevail and the arable land to be turned into building plots for summer cottages, especially along the Danube. As a result, the inflow of coins from villagers dropped off. So now the situation in the field is very much different: in search of buried coins and other antiquities metal detectors are buzzing and archaeological layers being destroyed by the "searchers".

In the end, the contribution should be acknowledged of Velimir Čeleketić, a years-long friend of the Museum. For fifty years now, since 1954, he has been bringing to the Museum whatever he may discover on the right, Srem, bank of the Danube between Slankamen and Zemun. His recent gift is a unique antoninianus of Salonina, wife of the emperor Gallienus (253–268), which bears a cross, the earliest known occurrence of a Christian symbol on coins. No such piece has been registered in the numismatic literature worldwide.

The augmentation of the Collection has been accompanied by the study and publication of the coins whose context and significance are inseparable from the city's history. More than half the collection has thus been presented to the general and professional public, as the reader of this text will be able to see from the bibliography dealing with numismatic finds from the territory of Belgrade.

The area of Belgrade changed hands among several peoples and state formations. The systematization of the selected items and catalogue has taken this fact into account.

Thus, for example, the Ottoman period (1521–1807) shows a subdivision into the groups of many European currencies that circulated in Belgrade. A numismatic study covering a span of twenty-three centuries has required more than one approach. Each group of money in the catalogue, i.e. each period that is distinct in monetary sense, is illustrated with a dozen photographs. The intention of such presentation is to demonstrate the basic characteristics of each period in terms of currency, without seeking to show the entire issues, an impossible task for so long a span of time.

THE SCORDISCI
Third century BC – first century AD

After the arrival of Celts in the Middle Danube and Morava river valleys in the fourth century BC in due course conditions were formed for the development of a money economy. A La Tène people, the Celts introduced a series of novelties into the life of native populations not only in the territories they physically occupied but within the effective range of their influence. The land began to be tilled with an iron plough, pottery to be thrown on the potter's wheel and a variety of metal objects for everyday use to be produced. As to the change in ethnic terms, the native populations began to relocate or were assimilated by the newcomers. Having suffered defeat after the sack of the Greek shrine at Delphi in 279 BC, part of the retreating Celts settled in Srem, i.e. in the Danubian and Moravian part of present-day Serbia. They formed the nucleus of a group whose name is known from classical sources – the Scordisci. The area between the Sava and the Danube remained their heartland until the Roman conquest in the late first century BC.

They became familiar with money in contacts with Hellenistic and Roman traders, and with the first issues of their own in the second century BC they entered the sphere of money economy. The early monetary picture in the heartland of Scordisci can be obtained from numismatic finds, i.e. from archaeological contexts. In addition to Celtic or Scordiscan coins, quite frequently found are silver drachms (about 3.5 g) of the Ionian coastal cities Apollonia and Dyrrhachium. There also occur silver and bronze coins of Alexander the Great and his successors. To the same period belong oft-found Roman Republican denarii.

Considering that the first protagonists of a money economy on this soil, and thus in Belgrade, were the Celtic tribe of Scordisci, a brief overview of their coinage seems appropriate.

The first coinage of the eastern Celts, whose eastward expansion reached the Carpathians, imitates the tetradrachm (about 15 g) of Philip II of Macedon (359–336 BC) with Zeus' head on the obverse and a horse rider on the reverse. The Celts generally remained faithful to that type, but imitations of imitations appeared in time and so the inscription vanished, the weight dropped, the metal was debased and stylization oscillated – depending on the issuing group and its real economic and technological capacity.

The Scordisci began to mint their coins in the second century BC. To their early coinage belong the abovementioned copies of tetradrachms with a bearded head on the obverse (Zeus) and a horse and rider on the reverse. Of a somewhat later date are the coins with Zeus' cheek shaped as a ball and a markedly elongated nose. The examples from this group, named the Srem group after the region where they are found most frequently, were coined in two denominations: a larger and heavier (9–11 g), and a smaller and lighter (about 2.3 g), conditionally termed tetradrachm and drachm respectively. The decline of Scordiscan power becomes increasingly reflected in their coins. Their weights generally drop and the ratio of the two weights becomes disturbed, the silver content is reduced, and bronze begins to be struck. Associated with this period of their decline is also the small silver coinage known as minimi (0.2–0.5 g), struck at their centres along the right bank of the Danube in eastern Srem to meet the needs of a shrunken and dried-up market.

The Sordiscan coinage suggests a social dimension, leading us to presume a close-knit community and an economically unified territory. After the Roman conquest, even the slightest trace of their coinage disappears, despite the survival of their community on the right side of the Danube in Srem attested by the finds such as a Roman funerary monument referring to a Civitas Scordiscorum.

1 CELTS (Scordisci),
3rd/2nd century BC
Tetradrachm, silver, wt 12.40 g,
diam. 24 mm - Inv. no 7148

Having become familiar with money and its function as a medium of exchange in contacts with the Hellenistic world, the Celtic tribe of Scordisci soon began their own coinage. For as long as they coined money one basic feature of the prototype was retained: a head and horseman combination. This piece, known as the Banat type, is an early imitation of Philip II's tetradrachm. It bears, obverse, Zeus' bearded head and, reverse, a horseman. There is a small cross-shaped countermark on the horse's chest and three wedge-shaped marks (III) above its back.

2

SCORDISCI,
2nd/1st century BC
Drachm, Srem type, silver, wt 2.45 g,
diam. 15 mm - Inv. no 3010

This coin type is often found in Srem, where it was minted. It is characterized by representation in raised relief. The obverse head with a puffed-up cheek, long nose and simple beard depicts a personality rather than a deity. The prancing horse has a mane represented by a row of pellets and the rider's figure is reduced to a circle inscribed with a dot.

3 SCORDISCAN MINIMI,
late 1st century BC

Silver, wt 0.47 g,
diam. 7 mm
Inv. no 8402

3a

Silver, wt 0.45 g,
diam. 7 mm
Inv. no 8398

3b

Gold, wt 0.13 g,
diam. 3.5 mm
Inv. no 10316

3c

Towards the end of their independence and monetary activity, during the last few decades of the first century BC, the Scordisci minted small silver coins known as minimi. The Belgrade City Museum keeps 57 such pieces. This gold piece is a unique and hitherto unregistered phenomenon in Scordiscan coinage.

ATHENS, 4th century BC
Tetradrachm, silver,
wt 16.87 g, diam. 21.5 mm
Inv. no 7138 4

Among the oldest pieces found in the Belgrade area is the one recovered from Ugrinovačka Street in Zemun. The type was minted from 393 BC. The obverse bears the head of Athena, the goddess of wisdom and protectress of Athens. The reverse is the owl of Athens with, before it, the initial letters of the city's name ΑΘΕ and, behind, a crescent and olive branch.

5 ALEXANDER THE GREAT
(336–323 BC)
Drachm, silver, wt 4.25 g,
diam. 16 mm – Inv. no 8250

When the Macedonian kings took control of the rich mines in the north of Greece, large amounts of coins, in silver and gold, began to pour out. To the barbarian world and Celts the tetradrachm of Philip II became the embodiment of coinage and a model to follow. This piece is a drachm of Alexander the Great showing the head of young Heracles (perhaps Alexander himself) with a lion's skin headdress on the obverse. The reverse is the chief god of the Hellenic world, Zeus enthroned, with an eagle in the right hand and the sceptre in the left. The inscription behind him reads [ΑΛΕΞ] ΑΝΔΡ[ΟΥ].

6

PELLA (188–168 BC)
Bronze, wt 8 g,
diam. 19 mm
Inv. no 8253

Pella was the capital of the Macedonian kings. Its mint was active for years. From it come the coinages of Philip II and Alexander. In the early decades of the third century BC the Thracian king Lysimachus also had his coinage minted at Pella. Pella retained the privilege to mint its coins even after the Roman victory at Pydna in 168 BC. This piece belongs to that period. On the obverse is Athena's head, and on the reverse a grazing bull with the legend ΠΕΛ above and ΛΕΣ below.

7 APOLLONIA,
2nd/1st century BC Drachm,
silver, wt 3.20 g, diam. 19 mm
Inv. no 8563

Coins of the Greek cities Apollonia and Dyrrhachium are found frequently in Scordiscan Belgrade, as evidenced by a large hoard discovered in the village of Zaklopača near Belgrade. The drachms of the two cities were minted on a standard close to that of the Roman republican denarius. The obverse shows Alcinous' gardens in the form of squares with convex sides and the inscription ΑΠΟΛ and ΝΙΚΙΑ. On the obverse is a cow and suckling calf, and above it the moneyer's name ΚΑΛΛΙ/ΣΤΡΑΤΟ[Σ].

ROMAN REPUBLICAN
issue of 103 BC
Denarius, silver, wt 3.95 g,
diam. 19.5 mm – Inv. no 7535 | 8

Roman trade cleared the way for its goods beyond the frontiers of the Empire. The proficient and persistent traders may be said to have traced the route for Roman conquests. The finds of Roman republican denarii in the Danube Basin belong to Scordiscan times. On the obverse of this piece is the head of Mars, the god of war, and, on the reverse, a Roman legionary fighting with barbarians. The legend reads Q·TERM·M· (the moneyer's name Q. Minucius).

THE ROMAN IMPERIAL PERIOD

First – mid-fifth centuries

The Roman military campaigns in the late first century BC mark the beginning of a new phase in the Danube Basin. Through these conquests the vast Empire accomplished its strategic aims. The Rhine and the Danube became borders separating the Roman world from the barbarians. The two powerful European rivers, however, could not function as a secure enough defence in themselves, and the Romans immediately set out to build a system of forts and observation posts along their banks. Thus in Belgrade, Roman Singidunum, a military encampment was put up in a suitable strategic place, present-day Kalemegdan. It was enclosed by a stonewall under the Emperor Trajan (98–117). After a series of different legions stationed on a short-term basis, the 4th Flavian legion was garrisoned in the fort from the late first century to the Hunnic invasion of 441, marking the end of the period of Antiquity on this soil. Nearby Viminacium (modern Kostolac) accommodated the 7th Claudian legion. The presence of two legions stationed so close to one another throughout the Roman period testifies to the importance of the roads and natural resources they controlled. A via militaris connecting the eastern and western parts of the Empire ran through Singidunum and Viminacium and continued along the Morava valley to Naissus (modern Niš). Another major communication was the Danube, leading towards the Roman cities on the Black Sea coast. The 4th Flavian legion controlled the mines on Mt Kosmaj, and the 7th Claudian those at Bor and Majdanpek. These data are important to understanding the economy, development and continuity of Singidunum, growing at the side of a large military camp. Different aspects of its urban life, including the town's administration and all benefits it offered to its inhabitants, are evidenced by copious finds of the material culture.

Next to the Roman camp in Kalemegdan the Roman town of Singidunum began to develop. In the last 150 years since the beginning of the recording of finds testifying to Belgrade's antique past, it has been established that Singidunum occupied the modern city's central zone, stretching from Kalemegdan towards Trg Republike and the Federal Parliament building. The abundant collection of artefacts from the time of Roman Singidunum has been enriched with gold, silver and bronze coins. Coins are usually found in structural remains, in graves as grave goods (the location of three Roman necropolises is known), and in vessels as a stored wealth whose owner vanished in a war taking with him the secret about the place the treasure had been buried. One of the largest hoards of Roman silver coins (2810 denarii and antoniniani) was found in Cara Uroša Street.

The economy and urban development of Singidunum under Roman rule relied on the fact that the 4th Flavian legion was garrisoned in Kalemegdan. The legionaries' good wages gave impetus to the development of crafts and created conditions for a civil settlement to emerge and grow. Singidunum was not only a post on the military road, but also a commercial channel. It was a frontier town of the Roman Empire on a powerful waterway – the Danube. It is in that light that its position in the huge Roman Empire should be viewed, above all as a major strategic point whose survival was ensured by the presence of a military force both under the Romans and in the subsequent centuries.

It is justly said that the circulation of Roman coins in Singidunum was high and frequent, as convincingly evidenced by numerous finds. Almost all kinds of coins are reported, and from all mints, which from the mid-third century began to be set up throughout the Empire. Singidunum has also yielded coins issued by some cities. Such issues are termed autonomous or local coinages. The operation of local mints was authorized by the emperor and their coinages fully fitted into the Empire's monetary system both metrically and iconographically. Smaller denominations were struck in bronze and their obverses almost always bore the emperor's portrait and inscription. In the eastern part of the Empire, owing to the Hellenistic tradition, a large number of cities continued their own coinages into the Roman period. Frequent finds in Belgrade of coins issued by Pontic and Anatolian cities – especially Nicaea, a recruitment centre in Bythinia – are related to the presence of craft products of eastern origin, recognizable in the recovered archaeological assemblages. In the 240s the inflow of Pontic and Anatolian coins all but ceased, the local coinage of Viminacium issued between 239 and 254/5 taking precedence.

The decline of the Roman Empire, undermined by disintegrating processes and increasingly frequent onslaughts by populations outside the Roman realm, was accompanied by the weakening of its economy and the interruption of travelling and trading networks. The Hunnic invasion of 441 under Attila, in which many towns and forts in the Danube Basin were destroyed, marked the end of Roman Singidunum.

VESPASIAN (AD 69–79)
Aureus, gold,
wt 7.20 g, diam. 18 mm
Inv. no 2118 9

The obverse shows the Emperor's laureate head and the inscription [IMP C] VESPASIAN [VS AVG]. On the reverse is the god of war Mars with a spear and trophy (the arms seized from the enemy), and the inscription along the rim MA [RS] – CONSERV [AT]. The gold aureus was the highest denomination. The value of all other coins, silver and bronze, was based on it. In the first 250 years of the Empire, before the silver denarius began to be debased, one aureus was equal to 25 denarii. From the end of the second century its weight was 7.40 g, or 1/45 of a Roman pound (327.45 g). During the third century the aureus steadily dropped in weight until Diocletian (284–305) stabilized it at 5.56 g (1/60 of a pound). A smaller hoard containing 12 coin types, including this aureus of Vespasian, was found in the nineteenth century near Batal Mosque, in whose place now stands the Federal Parliament building.

10 DOMITIAN (81–96)
Sestertius, orichalcum, wt 25.70 g, diam. 34 mm
Inv. no 1100

The obverse shows the Emperor's laureate head surrounded by the inscription CAES DIVI AVG VESP F DOMITIANVS COS VII. The reverse is the god of war Mars with a spear and trophy, flanked by the letters S and C. The Emperor Octavian Augustus' monetary reform at the beginning of his rule (23 BC) set the base-metal coinage into some order. Its issuance was placed under the charge of the Senate and hence the reverse abbreviation S–C, standing for Senatus Consulto (by order of the Senate). The heaviest and most valuable was the sestertius (27.28 g). Its half was the dupondius (12.5 g), while copper included the as (10.5 g) and its fractional denominations triens and quadrans. With debasement of silver, base-metal coins also began to drop in weight. When the silver coinage became so debased that it contained only 3–4 % silver, the senatorial issues were drastically reduced and eventually ceased to be minted in the 270s. Larger in size, sestertii and dupondii offered exceptional possibilities for conveying propagandistic messages, and the emperors did not fail to make the best use of the opportunity.

TRAJAN (98–117)
Denarius, silver,
wt 2.95 g, diam. 19 mm
Inv. no 884

11

The Roman emperors often commemorated their victories by adding the names of the defeated or subjugated to their names. If read carefully, this obverse inscription IMP TRAIANO AVG GER DAC P M TR P can reveal that the Emperor had subjugated Germania and Dacia, and thus became entitled to add the epithets Germanicus and Dacicus to his name. During his Dacian campaigns Trajan passed through Singidunum twice. In order to beat the Iron Gate rapids, he had a road cut through the rocks and a bridge across the Danube built. The reverse shows the seated personification of Equitas holding a balance and cornucopia, while its legend reads COS V PP SPQR OPTIMO PRINC. The initial weight of the silver denarius was about 3.4 g (1/96 of a Roman pound).

12 GORDIAN III (238–244)
Large bronze, local coinage,
Viminacium, wt 16.59, diam. 31 mm
S. Dušanić Collection, Inv. no 157

With the setting up of a local mint at Viminacium in 239, the bronze struck at other mints almost vanished from the Singidunum market. The Viminacium coinage became predominant, struck in three denominations equal to the senatorial sestertius, dupondius and as in their respective weights. This was the only Roman mint in the territory of present-day Serbia. The obverse of this piece shows the Emperor's bust surrounded by the legend IMP GORDIANVS PIVS FEL AVG. The reverse bears the standing figure of a young woman, personification of the province of Moesia. She is flanked by a bull, the emblem of the 7th Claudian legion stationed at Viminacium, and a lion, the emblem of the 4th Flavian legion based at Singidunum. The inscription is still more revealing: P M S C O–L VIM, meaning Provincia Moesia Superior Colonia Viminacium. The exergue contains AN III, meaning that the piece was struck in the third year of the local, Viminacium, era, beginning in October 239. Hence we know it was struck in 242/3, information of great interest to classical historians and archaeologists. Viminacium issued coins until 254/5, i.e. for sixteen years of the local era.

GALLIENUS (253–268)
Quinarius aureus, gold,
wt 1.61, diam. 18 mm
Inv. no 231

13

The obverse shows the Emperors' cuirassed and laureate bust surrounded by the inscription GALLIENVS AVG. The reverse inscription SECVRIT PERP[ET] accompanies the figure of a standing woman leaning against a column and holding the sceptre, personification of Securitas, perpetual security and safety. The coin, issued from the Rome mint, was found in a Roman tomb in King Alexander Street in Belgrade. The interest and importance of this coin lies in the fact that no such example has been recorded in the numismatic literature. The reverse legend and mintmark H, standing for the Rome mint of the period, reveals that the piece is a hybrid; namely, the reverse may have been struck with the die for another denomination, the silver antoninianus.

14 SALONINA (253–268)
Antoninianus, bronze,
silver-washed, wt 2.30 g,
diam. 21 mm – Inv. no 9433

The obverse shows the Empress and the inscription SALONINA AVG, while on the reverse is the enthroned goddess of the hearth and the surrounding legend VESTA. The top of her diadem, proper to an empress, identifies Vesta with the Empress Salonina, wife of the Emperor Gallienus. In her right hand Vesta, i.e. the Empress, holds the cross with its arms in the form of pellets. In her left hand is a cruciform sceptre. This is another unique piece given that this was the first time that an official document, which a coin is, showed a Christian symbol – the cross. It was struck in 265, four years after Gallienus' edict of religious toleration (261) and some fifty years before the Edict of Milan, recognizing Christianity. Such a piece has not been registered in the numismatic literature. It was found in the environs of Belgrade, at Dobanovci.

15

PROBUS (276–282)
Antoninianus, bronze,
silver-washed, wt 3.20 g,
diam. 23 mm – Inv. no 383

The obverse shows the Emperor with a radiate crown, an element of this coin type, and the legend IMP C M AVG PROBVS AVG. His cuirassed bust is draped in a lavish cloak and he holds in the right hand the sceptre with an eagle perched on its tip. The reverse bears the inscription ROMAE AETERNAE, Roma seated in a temple, holding Victoria, the goddess of victory, in the right hand and the sceptre in the left. The letters in the exergue stand for the Rome mint (R) and one of its workshops (S). Probus' antoniniani are characterized by high-quality silvering. Although struck at a number of imperial mints, his issues show standardized weights, testifying to a centralized and disciplined functioning of the huge Empire's monetary system.

16 JULIAN OF PANNONIA,
usurper emperor (283–285)
Aureus, gold, wt 5 g,
diam. 21 mm – Inv. no 2437

In the militarily and politically tumultuous year 283 Julian the Pannonian usurped the throne and had himself proclaimed emperor. He immediately issued coinage in his own name, thereby asserting himself as a new ruler. But his power did not extend beyond Pannonia and he had in his hands the mint at Siscia (modern Sisak, Croatia). He issued just one gold series. The obverse shows the usurper's bust and name IMP C IVLIANVS P F AVG. The reverse bears the inscription LIBERTAS PVBLICA and its personification: the standing figure of a young woman holding a bag in the right hand and a cornucopia in the left.

DIOCLETIAN (284–305) 17
Follis, bronze,
wt 8.30 g, diam. 28 mm
Inv. no 1331

The obverse shows the Emperor's laureate head surrounded by the inscription IMP C DIOCLETIANVS P F AVG. The reverse shows the Genius of the Roman people symbolized by a young man holding a patera and cornucopia, as well as the legend GENIO POPVLI ROMANI and the mintmark *SIS (Siscia/Sisak). The weakened Empire with its vitiated institutions was brought back to life by the soldier emperors of Illyrian origin Claudius Gothicus, Aurelian and Probus. It was them that had largely paved the way for Diocletian's reorganization of the state hitherto based on the principate system of government. He administratively divided the Empire into four parts ruled by two augusti and two caesars, and for that reason this system is known as tetrarchy. In 294 Diocletian carried out a coinage reform on which the Empire's monetary system would continue to be based, with minor modifications. The gold aureus was stabilized and the silver argentus and bronze nummus introduced. We know the latter as follis, named after the bags into which coins were packed for distribution. Folles were struck at all mints of the Empire.

18 CONSTANTINE I (306–337)
1½-solidus multiple, gold,
wt 6.75, diam. 23 mm
Inv. no 2435

The solidus was introduced by Constantine the Great in 309. Its weight of 4.55 g (1/72 of a Roman pound) remained stable over the centuries. In later times, it was adopted as the Byzantine gold standard. In the early phase of its minting it sometimes bears the mark of value LXXII or OB (perhaps the Greek number 72 or the abbreviation for obrussa = fire-tested). The value of this piece is 1.5 solidi. The obverse shows the Emperor's bust and the inscription IMP CONTANTINVS MAX AVG, while the reverse bears the sun-god Sol and the legend SOLI INVI–CTO COMITI. The mintmark is SIS (Siscia). This gold piece with its legend celebrating the god Sol reveals the state of religious affairs at the time of its minting (317). Christianity was not to become a state religion until after the Council of Nicaea, called and opened by the Emperor Constantine himself in 325. The coin formed part of a smaller hoard of gold coins found in the village of Ušće near Obrenovac.

VALENTINIAN (364–378)
Solidus, gold,
wt 4.51 g, diam. 22 mm
Inv. no 2178

19

This solidus of Valentinian testifies to a stable production of gold coinage in spite of difficulties and increasingly frequent barbarian attacks on the Empire's frontiers. The obverse shows the Emperor's name DN VALENTINI–ANVS PF AVG and his laureate, cuirassed and draped bust. The reverse depicts the Emperor as the restorer of the state, as suggested by the legend RESTITVTOR–REI PVBLICAE. He holds a labarum with the monogram of Christ in his right hand, and a globe in the left, while being crowned by Victoria. The exergue contains SMNI (the mint of Nicomedia).

20 VALENS (364–378)
Siliqua, silver,
wt 1.80 g, diam. 17 mm
Inv. no 558

Silver was rarely coined during the late Empire. This piece shows the Emperor's bust surrounded by the inscription DN VALEN–S P F AVG. On the reverse is seated Roma on a backed throne holding Victoria on the globe and a sceptre. The design is accompanied by the inscription VRBS–ROMA and the mintmark TRPS (Trier). In 324 Constantine the Great introduced the silver siliqua, but its standard weight of 2.60 g soon began to drop. Its production was slightly intensified in the second half of the fourth century, which is the period that this piece belongs to.

THE BYZANTINE PERIOD

End of the fifth – early thirteenth centuries

Throughout the millennium-long life of the Byzantine Empire, the frontier town of Belgrade shared its fate. After the devastating Hunnic invasion of 441, Roman Singidunum was a deserted place. Gradually consolidating its rule following the fifth-century wave of migrations, Byzantium regained military and administrative control of its northern frontier on the Danube. For nearly eleven centuries that the Empire, heir to the classical and Christian civilization, was in existence, coins were minted. For the monetary system of a country that is a very long time, necessarily marked by many social and economic changes. All the changes reflected in its coinage.

In political terms, Byzantium was formed in 395, when the Roman Empire was divided into its western and eastern halves. The former collapsed in 476, whereas the end of the latter, Byzantium, was marked by the fall of its capital Constantinople to the Ottoman Turks in 1453. During the fifth century the monetary systems of both parts of the Roman Empire were based on the traditions and legacy of Rome. Solidi were struck from fine gold, while silver was rarely coined. In the difficult mid-century, under barbarian onslaughts against both parts of the Empire, bronze virtually ceased to be coined except for the nummus, small both in size and in weight (about 1 g).

The monetary cohesion of the divided Empire was brought to an end by the Byzantine Emperor Anastasius (491–518). He carried out a radical monetary reform in 498 and introduced a new bronze unit – the follis. Its initial weight of about 9 g soon increased to no less than 22 g. The newly-introduced denomination, unusually heavy and large by comparison to the bronze coinage struck at the time, was well received and highly prized. Its reverse bore the Greek numeral M standing for 40 (nummi). Its fractions were also coined, themselves with the marks of value: K (20 nummi), I (10 nummi) and E (5 nummi). Less frequently their values were also expressed in Roman numerals. The Anastasian reforms may be taken as the beginning of almost millennium-long Byzantine coinage. The gold solidus with an average weight of 4.5 g remained the basic unit and all silver and bronze was based on it. There were also fractional gold denominations worth a half and a third of a solidus, known as the semissis and the tremissis respectively.

In a revived economy under Anastasius I, and particularly during the renewal under Justinian in the first half of the sixth century, the newly-introduced bronze denominations reached the busy area of Byzantine Singidunum. Justinian renovated the entire system of Roman forts along the Danube, demolished or deserted in the fifth century. The fortress in Kalemegdan was also renovated, though now somewhat smaller in size than the Roman one. As a Byzantine military base in the following decades, Singidunum was important for the defence of the northern frontier and functioned as an observation point for controlling the movement of barbarian peoples. Concurrently with this restoration of the country's defences, civilian life was also being restored. Trade and crafts began to recover, as evidenced by the presence of sixth-century coinage struck from almost all mints.

Early in the seventh century, under the Emperor Heraclius (610–641), the Danube Basin saw the settlement of Slavic tribes, Serbs among them, whose recorded presence in the Belgrade area reaches back to about 630. The Slavic name of our city – Beograd (White Fortress) – was first recorded in 878.

The ninth and tenth centuries, when the area was under Bulgarian rule, are still marked by a predominance of Byzantine coinage.

The arrival and settlement of Hungarians in the Pannonian Plain posed a threat to the Byzantine northern border. The entire twelfth century was marked by struggles for control over the Danube. The presence of the Emperor Manuel Comnenus in person (1143–80) in Belgrade in 1151 and his fights with the Hungarians in Srem reveal the importance of the region for the Empire as a whole. Byzantium eventually gave up Belgrade and Danubian Serbia in the late twelfth century; still, Byzantine coins, both gold and bronze, continued to circulate in the area. They are known as cup money for their cuplike shape. The finds have been recorded, if not always preserved, of several thousand pieces of such bronze. It is such sizeable assemblages–hoards that testify to the turbulent times in which they were stored away.

21 ANASTASIUS (491–518)
Follis, bronze,
wt 19.5 g, diam. 35 mm
Inv. no 6 (Hoard P)

During the reign of Anastasius Belgrade was firmly in Byzantine hands and the Empire's northern border was well controlled, while under Justinian I the renovation began of major strategic points. A strong military presence considerably stimulated trade and crafts, as inferable from the finds of coins issued by Anastasius and the subsequent sixth-century rulers. The year 498 may be seen as the beginning of Byzantine coinage, as Anastasius carried out a monetary reform and introduced a new bronze unit, the 40-nummus follis. He broke with traditional Roman types and Christian motifs took over instead. On the obverse of this follis is the Emperor's bust surrounded by the inscription DN ANASTA–SIVS PP AVG, while the centre of the reverse shows a large M (= 40 nummi), a cross, two stars, and the letter B as the mark of series. The exergue contains the mintmark CON (Constantinople).

ANASTASIUS (491–518)
Tremissis, gold,
wt 1.38 g, diam. 14 mm
Inv. no 236

22

From 324 in addition to the gold solidus, lower gold denominations began to be coined, the semissis (1/2 of a solidus) and tremissis (1/3). Anastasius retained this ratio in his monetary reform. The obverse of this tremissis shows the Emperor's bust accompanied by the inscription DN ANASTA–SIVS PP AVG. The reverse depicts Victoria advancing with a wreath in one hand and the globe surmounted by a cross in the other. The inscription reads: VICTORIA AVGUSTORVM. The exergue contains CONOB (Constantinople mint).

23 JUSTINIAN I (527–565)
Solidus, gold,
wt 4.38 g, diam. 21 mm
Inv. no 2440

The Emperor Justinian compiled all the Roman and Byzantine laws into a huge corpus that has survived till this day. Justinian was a great statesman as well. During his long reign, he consolidated the northern Danube frontier, renovated the forts and breathed fresh life into the weakened economy. His coins are often found in Belgrade. The obverse of this gold piece shows the Emperor holding a cross and the surrounding inscription DN IVSTINI–ANVS PP AVG. On the reverse is the standing figure of Victoria, holding a long cross in the right hand and the globe surmounted by a cross in the left. The inscription reads VICTORIA–AVCCCS. The exergue contains CONOB (Constantinople mint).

MAURICE TIBERIUS (582–602)
Solidus, gold,
wt 4.52 g, diam. 21 mm
Inv. no 1014 24

Many Byzantine coins show a combination of Latin and Greek lettering, as shown by this example. The obverse depicts the Emperor's cuirassed bust facing, with a feathered headdress. He holds the globe surmounted by a cross in his right hand and a shield with a horseman in the right. He is surrounded by the legend DN MAVR–TIb PP AVI. The reverse shows the standing figure of Victoria, holding a long staff surmounted by the monogram of Christ in her right hand and the globe surmounted by a cross in the left. The figure is framed by the inscription VICTORIA–AVCC$_{B}$. The exergue contains CONOB (Constantinople mint).

25 CONSTANTINE VII
and ROMANUS II (945–959)
Solidus, gold, wt 4.34 g,
diam. 21 mm – Inv. no 75

In contrast with the shaky economy of the Empire and a relative lack of lower bronze denominations, the gold coinage was sound. This obverse shows the busts of the issuing emperors holding a patriarchal cross between them, with another cross above each head. A barely legible inscription runs around them. The reverse shows the haloed bust of Christ holding the Gospels in his left hand. The surrounding legend reads IhSXPS REX REGNA TIЧM. The coin was struck at Constantinople.

26

BASIL II (976–1025)
Anonymous follis, bronze,
wt 10.20, diam. 27 mm
Inv. no 2340

The seventh century was marked by Avaro-Slavic and Persian onslaughts. The economic and money flows almost dried up, and the entire eight century was a period of crisis the Byzantine Empire had to cope with. Gold was coined in reduced quantities but there was no debasement. The bronze follis underwent several reductions, its weight dropped considerably and its production was slimmed down. At the time of economic renewal under Basil II in the late tenth century the sound bronze coinage of about 10 g began to be struck. It significantly helped to restore the flow of money and goods. This piece was found on the right side of the Danube downstream from Belgrade. The obverse shows the bust of Christ holding the Gospels, flanked by IC and XC. The inscription +EMMA–NOVHΛ runs around him. The entire reverse is inscribed with IhSЧS / XPISTЧS / bASILEЧ / bASILE.

27 MANUEL COMNENUS
(1143–80)
Nomisma, electrum, wt 3.95 g,
diam. 28 mm – Inv. no 2975

In the late eleventh century Byzantine coinage underwent a change. The gold unit was named nomisma, given a cuplike shape and generally struck in electrum (mixture of gold and silver). The same cup shape, the main feature of Byzantine coinage between the eleventh and thirteenth centuries, was given to the bronze coinage as well. The eleventh and twelfth centuries saw Byzantium and Hungary frequently struggling for control over the Danube Basin. Under Manuel Comnenus the Fortress of Belgrade was renovated, enlarged and heavily garrisoned. The Emperor made a stay in Belgrade twice, extending his military operations into Zemun and Srem. A few large hoards of cup money discovered in the area are a reflection of war-related insecurity. On the obverse of this nomisma issued by Manuel are the Emperor and St Theodore standing side by side. They hold between them the patriarchal cross on a globe. The reverse depicts the standing figure of Christ, blessing with his right hand and holding the Gospels in the left. His head is flanked by the letters IC and XC.

THE HUNGARIAN COINAGE
Thirteenth century – 1521

For the good part of the medieval period Belgrade was within the Hungarian realm. The Kingdom of Hungary struggled bitterly with Byzantium for control over the Danube Basin, especially in the second half of the twelfth century. A Byzantine border fort, Belgrade was an exposed target. Hungary took control of the town about 1230. Apart from two shorter periods of Serbian rule, in 1284–1319 and 1403/4–1427, it remained in its hands until the Ottoman conquest in 1521.

By the mid-fifteenth century, when preparations for defence against the Ottomans began, Hungary had left no visible trace on the city's urban plan. The discovered coins of its kings, indeed few or completely lacking, reveal the same picture. Its presence south of the Sava and Danube rivers may be to an extent deduced from the recurrent toponym "Hungarian cemetery" (Lajkovac, Smederevo, a few in the Obrenovac area), but it cannot be dated.

Hungary began to mint its own coinage quite early, in the reign of its first King Stephen (1000–38), founder of the Árpád dynasty, which held the Hungarian throne for three whole centuries, until 1307. This coinage, with minor exceptions, was mainly in silver. The initial issue was that of denars, about 1.3 g in weight. The number of types gradually increased and smaller silver pieces were introduced, the obol and half-denar (0.5–0.6 g). The obols and half-denars issued by the Árpád rulers have been found in large quantities on several sites in Zemun. The reverses of those issued by the kings Koloman (1095–1114), Stephen II (1114–31) and Béla (1131–41) show the inscription LADISLAVS RE(X). Pieces issued by other Hungarian kings have also been found. The abundance and proximity of the finds of the obols of these kings gives grounds to assume that an amount of this money is likely to be expected in Belgrade as well.

The issuance of bronze scyphati, cup-shaped coins, by King Stephen IV (1162–63) constitutes an interesting phenomenon in Hungarian coinage. They are similar to the Byzantine scyphati of the time in shape and designs. The similarity is understandable given that the Byzantine Emperor Manuel I Comnenus supported Stephen's usurpation of the Hungarian throne in 1162.

With King Charles I, Robert of Anjou (1307–42), Hungarian coinage entered a new phase, which lasted until Hungary's defeat by the Ottomans at the Battle of Mohács in 1526. He issued a larger silver of the gros type and began to coin in gold. The gold coinage was struck on the model of the Florentine florin, indeed was identical to it except for the addition of King Charles's name.

The gold coins of King Sigismund (1411–37) received the emblems of Brandenburg (eagle) and Bohemia (lion), parts of his realm. Between 1446 and 1453 Hungarian coins bear the name of János Hunyadi, known as Sibinjanin

Janko from Serbian folk poems. The legend GU–BERNATOR UNGARIE signifies his office as governor of Hungary, regent for underage Ladislas V who acceded to the throne in 1453. The coinage of Matthias Corvinus (1458–90) shows the Virgin with the legend PATRONA UNGARIAE. This design occurs later on the gold coins of Vladislas II (1490–1516), in whose reign the Hungarian thaler began to be coined for the first time.

After the defeat at Mohács in 1526 and the Ottoman capture of Buda in 1541, the Hungarian crown went to the Austrian archduke Ferdinand (1526–64). For that reason the coinage the newly-formed Austro-Hungarian union issued after 1526 will be presented in the following chapter dealing with the Ottoman period, as a currency of the state that now controlled the area of present-day Belgrade.

28 KOLOMAN (1095–1114)
Obol, silver,
wt 0.60 g, diam. 12 mm
Inv. no 8655

Around the obverse cross potent runs the name of the ruler in slanting letters +CA–L–M–N. The reverse shows another cross, with a pellet in each quarter, surrounded by the inscription +LADISLAVS RE.

29 BÉLA II (1131–41)
Obol, silver,
wt 0.37 g, diam. 11 mm
Inv. no 8660

The obverse shows three crosses separated by semicircles and a pellet in the centre. The reverse shows the cross inscribed in a slightly raised ring. The design is surrounded by the illegible slanting lettering.

STEPHEN IV (1162–63) 30
Scyphatus, bronze,
wt 3.50 g, diam. 26 mm
Inv. no 8665

Stephen IV acceded to the Hungarian throne in 1162 amply supported by the Byzantine Emperor Manuel I Comnenus. An echo of that support can be seen in this cup-shaped coin that Stephen IV issued under the direct influence, or rather as a copy, of the Byzantine scyphatus. The obverse shows the inscription REX BELA–REX STS surrounding Béla II and Stephen IV each seated on his throne and holding a sword and the globe surmounted by a cross, with the mark III in the exergue. The reverse shows the enthroned Virgin with Christ, with a cross at either side of her head and the legend SANCTA–MARIA.

BÉLA IV (1235–70) 31
Denar, silver,
wt 0.72 g, diam. 14.5 mm
Inv. no 8741

The reverse shows the emblem of Slavonia, a marten running left between two stars. The design is surrounded by the inscription MONETA + REGIS P SCLAVONIA+. The obverse cross is flanked by two confronted and diademed heads, with a star above one and a crescent above the other.

32 SIGISMUND (1387–1437)
Ducat, gold,
wt 3.55 g, diam. 20 mm
Inv. no 566

In 1411 the Holy Roman emperor Sigismund became king of Hungary. The obverse of this Hungarian gold shows a shield surrounded by the legend +SIGISMVNDI·G·R·VNGARIE. The obverse depicts the standing figure of St Ladislas holding an axe in the right hand and the globe surmounted by a cross in the left. The figure is surrounded by the inscription S·LADISL·AVS·REX.

33 MATTHIAS CORVINUS
(1458–90)
Ducat, gold, wt 4 g,
diam. 21 mm – Inv. no 2193

The obverse shows a shield charged with heraldic devices and the inscription +MATHIAS·D·G·R·VNGARIE running along the rim. The obverse bears the standing figure of St Ladislas, holding a high-raised sword in the right hand and the globe surmounted by a cross in the left. The inscription reads ·S·LADISL–AVS·REX.

THE MEDIEVAL SERBIAN COINAGE

Thirteenth – fifteenth centuries

Belgrade first passed into the hands of a Serbian ruler in 1284, when Ladislas IV of Hungary granted present-day northern Serbia with Belgrade to Dragutin (King of Raška 1276–82, Lord of Srem 1284–1316), married to his sister Katalin. Dragutin's residence was at Debrc. A piece of information of interest for the territory under his rule, where his coinage was in use, is that he controlled the mines on Mt Rudnik, where his mint was set up. In 1319, a few years after his death, the Hungarians took back his realm, Belgrade included.

Almost a century later, between 1403/4 and 1427, Belgrade was once more in the hands of a Serbian ruler, Despot Stefan Lazarević (*knez* or prince, 1389–1402; despot, 1402–27), who moved his residence from Kruševac to Belgrade. After the Despot's death in 1427, according to a previous agreement made at Tata, Belgrade was restored to Hungary. Despot Djuradj Branković, Stefan's nephew, made the newly built fortress of Smederevo his capital.

The first rulers of Raška, beginning with the grand *župan* Stefan Nemanja (1166–95), expanded their realm at the expense of its suzerain, the Byzantine Empire. They did not coin money.

Serbian coinage began with King Radoslav, the eldest son of Stefan the First Crowned. His wife was Anna, daughter of Theodore I of Epirus. His coinage was in silver and copper, cup-shaped, typologically identical to the Byzantine coinage of the period. Radoslav's coins were scarce and exerted no influence on the issues of subsequent rulers of Raška that were to appear soon, in more favourable circumstances and on the model of the Venetian matapan in terms of type and size. Medieval Serbian rulers did not coin in gold.

Stefan Uroš I (King, 1243–76) was the youngest son of Stefan the First Crowned and Anna Dandolo, daughter of a Venetian doge. His wife was Jelena (Helene) of Anjou. He fostered the development of the country's economy and by recruiting skilful Saxon miners gave impetus to mining and trade. Silver became and remained Raška's staple export commodity. Typologically, Uroš I's silver coinage is very similar to the Venetian matapan, except that the latter's legend DVX (doge) running vertically along the banner staff the saint is handing over to the doge is replaced with REX (king) both in the coinage of Uroš and in the same coin type issued by his successors. Uroš's coinage is not reliably distinguishable from that of his sons, Dragutin and Milutin. The matapan inscribed with the name STEFANVS is considered to belong to Uroš. The subsequent Serbian rulers continued to rely on the coinages of Uroš and his sons, introducing new designs, until the fall of the Despotate of Serbia to the Turks in 1459.

For nearly 250 years of the medieval Serbian state and its coinage, a large number of different types or designs have been registered. In the early kingdom predominates the obverse bareheaded or diademed ruler receiving the cross or a standard from St Stephen. The reverses show Christ enthroned holding the Gospels. One type of Dragutin's coins is the enthroned king with a sword resting on his knees and the cruciform sceptre in the right hand (type that was to reappear later). Another type, also Dragutin's, shows the King's name written in Cyrillic script for the first time: СТЕФАN РАБЍ ХυО. The coronation series of King and Emperor Dušan (1331–55), proclaimed emperor in 1345 and crowned a year later at Skopje, shows him being crowned by two angels. This type is particularly interesting, and praiseworthy from the perspective of the propagandistic use of coinage. The design can be seen on earlier Byzantine coinage showing the ruler being crowned by two Victorias, investing him with royal power and the crown of invincibility. By reiterating this motif, the Emperor Dušan laid claim to the throne of a restored Byzantine Empire. Dušan issued many different types. On some, and ever more frequently, we can see the empress standing next to the emperor instead of the patron saint. There also occur the emperor's equestrian portrait, conveying a symbolism of victory, and diverse floral motifs. Dušan introduced a smaller denomination of about 0.70 g struck with various types.

Equally varied was the coinage of the Despot Stefan Lazarević who, in a relatively short time after the Battle of Kosovo in 1389, consolidated the country and created an inspiring environment for cultural developments. The consolidation is reflected in his coinage, beautiful and diverse, with its weight stabilized at about 1g. More than 70 types of his coins are known. Motifs are varied. The reverses often bear the Despot's name and title.

Several coins of almost all medieval Serbian rulers have so far been recovered from the territory of Belgrade. The collection includes both coins found in hoards that were secreted away and individual finds.

STEFAN UROŠ I
(King of Raška, 1243–76)
Dinar, silver, wt 1.75 g,
diam. 20 mm – Inv. no 406

34

King Uroš I coined his silver on the model of Venetian matapans. He was tied by marriage with the Venetian doge Dandolo. With that, and a strong Venetian interest in the rich mines on Mt Rudnik in mind, his decision to follow the Venetian example may be seen as a response to the needs of trade. The reign of Uroš I is characterized by a prosperous economy. By bringing skilful Saxon miners to Serbia, he spurred the development of mining and trade. In a short time Raška became known for its silver, of the highest quality in Europe. The obverse of this dinar issued by Uroš I shows the bareheaded king and the saint holding a banner along the staff of which runs REX. The design is surrounded by the inscription VROSIVS–STEFAN. The reverse bears Christ enthroned with the Gospels in his lap.

35 DRAGUTIN (King of Raška, 1276–82;
Lord of Srem, 1284–1316)
Dinar, silver, wt 2.10,
diam. 21 mm – Inv. no 2983

The obverse shows the standing figure of the diademed king holding the cruciform sceptre in his right hand; two small crosses can be seen next to his left arm, and one next to the right. Cyrillic (Serbian) script used for the inscription, СТЕФАN – РАБЬ XυО (Stefan, a servant of Christ), expresses the administrative and political independence of his realm, the region of Srem and northern Serbia. The reverse shows the enthroned figure of Jesus Christ holding the Gospels in his lap with both hands. There is a cross on either side of the throne.

36

MILUTIN (King of Raška, 1282–1321) Dinar, wt 2.15 g, diam. 21 mm Inv. no 2539

Under King Milutin Raška witnessed a rise in every respect. He expanded his state to the south, towards Byzantium, and absorbed the northern region of Braničevo. Especially active were the mines of Brskovo, Novo Brdo and Rudnik. He was of those Raška rulers who pursued extensive building projects. He had the monasteries of Gračanica and Banjska built, while that of Hilandar on Mount Athos was extensively rebuilt. His coinage is homogeneous and quite heavy (over 2 g). Milutin introduced new types, designs (ruler's seated figure) and legends, such as VROSIVS REX or STEFAN REX. This piece shows the same obverse as the coin of Uroš I (ruler and saint) inscribed with VROSIVS–S STEFAN. The reverse bears Christ enthroned holding the Gospels.

37 DUŠAN (King, 1331–45; Emperor, 1345–55)
Dinar, silver, wt 1.60 g, diam. 22 mm – Inv. no 2998

During Dušan's reign as king and emperor, the Serbian state was at its peak. His state extended as far southwards as the Peloponnesus. His intention was to become the ruler of a restored Byzantine Empire. He issued many types in hundreds of varieties. In addition to the dinar, he coined half-dinars. He struck no bronze, which indicates that local markets were not developed. This piece belongs to his imperial period. Its obverse shows the Emperor's equestrian portrait as a symbol of victory. He holds the sceptre and cross. The inscription reads C Φ b – Z P (Stefan Emperor). The reverse is the bust of Christ blessing with one hand and holding a scroll in the other. Christ's head is flanked by IC and XC.

LAZAR HREBELJANOVIĆ 38
(Prince of the Serbian Lands, 1371–89)
Dinar, silver, wt 1.25 g, diam. 18.5 mm
Inv. no 9148

Dušan's son and heir Uroš V was incapable of preserving the cohesion of the Serbian state overwhelmed by a wave of decentralization. This fragmentation is clearly reflected in the coinages of local rulers, whether authorized to mint their coinage or usurpers. Prince Lazar (conte, as titled on one of his coin types) showed pretensions to the Nemanjić throne, through the line of his wife Milica. He issued several coin types, inscribed both in Cyrillic and Latin scripts. This dinar shows the enthroned ruler with the princely crown holding the sceptre and cross. His figure is flanked by the inscription К Н Е – З Ь / Л А – З Р Ь. The reverse shows Christ enthroned with the Gospels in his lap. The fragmentation of the Serbian state facilitated Ottoman penetration into the central Balkans after the death of Prince Lazar at the Battle of Kosovo in 1389.

39 STEFAN LAZAREVIĆ
(Despot, 1389–1427)
Dinar, silver, wt 0.75 g,
diam. 17 mm – Inv. no 2554

The obverse legend in the quarters of the cross runs in two courses: Д/Е/СП/ОТ. The reverse shows the standing figure of Christ enclosed in a mandorla. With his left hand he holds the Gospels against his chest and blesses with the right. Stefan Lazarević was granted the title of despot by the Byzantine emperor in Constantinople in 1402. A year later, 1403/4, he moved his residence to Belgrade, granted to him by Hungary. Thus Belgrade became the capital of a Serbian state for the first time. The Despot put new life into it in every respect. In a short time, Belgrade became a cultural centre. The Despot's court, in present-day Kalemegdan, was a focus for many learned men fleeing Byzantium before the advancing Ottoman armies.

40

DJURADJ BRANKOVIĆ
(Despot, 1427–56)
Dinar, silver, wt 1.13 g,
diam. 15 mm – Inv. no 1317

The obverse is inscribed with ГNbДE/CПOTb/ГИOPГb (Lord Despot Djurdje). The reverse shows a lion advancing left, emblem of the Vuković-Branković house, and the legend CMEДEPEBO (Smederevo), where the coin was minted. For almost thirty years of his rule, despite all the difficulties, the Despot minted diversely and extensively. His coins bear the names of mints such as Rudnik, Novo Brdo and Smederevo.

Dubrovnik and Venice

41 DUBROVNIK
issue of 1372–1421
Dinar, silver, wt 1.5 g,
diam. 19 mm – Inv. no 580

The obverse shows the standing figure of St Vlaho, the city's patron saint, clad as a bishop and haloed. He holds a staff in his left hand while blessing with the right. Round his image runs the inscription A·S·BASIV–S·RAGVSII. On the reverse is Christ enclosed in a mandorla and flanked by ID–XD (inverted letters). Dubrovnik maintained intense commercial contacts with its Balkan hinterland. It began to mint its own coinage at the end of the thirteenth century, continuing to do so until 1803, when the Republic ceased to exist. During these centuries it issued different coins of which dinars, half-dinars, little dinars and even thalers are found in Belgrade.

42

Republic of VENICE Matapan,
Doge Giovanni Soranzo (1312–28),
silver, wt 1.97 g,
diam. 19 mm – Inv. no 8653

The obverse shows St Mark presenting the banner to the doge. Along the banner staff runs the legend DVX, and the scene is surrounded with IO SVPANTIO–S M VENETI. The reverse depicts Christ enthroned flanked by IC–XC. The city-state of Venice began to grow in the ninth century and throughout its long existence played an important part in the flow of commerce in the Balkans. Venetian coinage began with the doge Vitale II Michielli (1156–72) continuing until 1797 when the Republic was abolished by Napoleon. Venetian coins almost always show St Mark, the city's patron saint, presenting the doge with the symbol of power, banner with a cross, as a God's blessing. As a result of large-scale commercial dealings, silver matapans and gold zecchini reached our parts. From Uroš I, the Serbian medieval coinage followed the model of the matapan. Predominant among the finds discovered in Belgrade and its environs are matapans and zecchini.

43 Republic of VENICE
Zecchino, Doge Francesco Foscari
(1423–1457), gold, wt 3.41,
diam. 20 mm – Inv. no 74

The obverse shows St Mark presenting the banner to the doge. On the left-hand side is the inscription ·S·M·VENETI, and on the right FRAN. FOSCARI. The reverse is inscribed with SIT·T·HPE·DAT·Q·TV REGIS ISTE DVCAT round the standing figure of Christ in a mandorla holding the Gospels in the left hand. The original and widespread name of this gold coin was ducat (from ducatus = duchy, as can be seen on coins). In 1284 it was renamed zecchino. It was from that year that it was minted at the palace La Zecchia, which gave it its name. The mint remained in the palace until the abolition of the Republic. Owing to its fineness, the zecchino was the preferred currency in the Balkans for a long time.

THE OTTOMAN PERIOD

1521–1878
Ottoman and European coinages

Seized by the Turks, Belgrade soon became an important military and trading centre in the Danube region of the vast Ottoman Empire. Throughout the period of Turkish rule – with intermittent episodes of Austrian domination (1688–91, 1717–39 and 1788–91) – and well into the nineteenth century, until 1878 when the autonomous Principality of Serbia became a sovereign state, Turkish money was used in Belgrade as a means of payment. This chapter will also present the currencies of other European states that circulated both for commercial reasons and due to the intermittent episodes of Austrian domination.

Turkish coinage began quite late, with the Sultan Orhan (1324–62). Those were small silver coins known as akçes or aspers. Akçes were coined all through to 1839 at many mints across the Empire. The first copper coin, mangır, was minted by the Sultan Murad I (1362–89), well known to us from the Battle of Kosovo. Finally, Mehmed II the Conqueror (1444–46 and 1451–81), the conqueror of Constantinople, Bosnia and Smederevo, began to coin in gold late in his reign in 1478. Minting in the three metals continued as long as the Ottoman Empire coined its money. In accordance with economic needs and potentials, new denominations were introduced and their weights altered.

Turkish coins were inscribed in Arabic script from the beginning until after the World War One, when Latin script was introduced under Atatürk. Thus their form remained virtually unchanged for some six centuries. As Islam banned the representation of human figures and images, ornaments and calligraphic inscriptions predominated. The elaborate and meticulously rendered tughra not only had the function to glorify the sultan but also to discourage forgery. Essentially, the Turkish coinage is very clear as it contains the basic data about the issuing authority – the sultan's name, title, father's name, first regnal year and the mint.

Belgrade's strategic position, enhanced by the Turkish advance into Europe, the fortress in Kalemegdan and the presence of troops, spurred its growth as a Turkish frontier town, which soon after the conquest in 1521 became an important trading centre within the Ottoman Empire. No more than fifty years later, in 1567, M. A. Pigafetta's account of his journey to Constantinople reveals the appearance of Belgrade. His description of the fortress and its location is so vivid that the reader has the impression of looking at an old engraving. But the account goes further, describing the outlying civilian settlement stretching towards the Danube, full of Turkish, Jewish and Serbian houses, and shops of merchants from Dubrovnik and other parts. It was a period preceding the rise of the grand vizier Mehmed Pasha Sokollu (Sokolović), who was to foster the growth of the town by having a roofed market, a caravansary and other buildings erected in the quarter known as Dorćol. Belgrade developed as a centre of crafts supplying the army. In the reign of Süleyman I (1520–66) silver and gold began to be struck at Belgrade (1562–66). No more than six gold pieces struck in his name at Belgrade are known. Silver coins – akçes, onluks and paras (smaller in size and weight) – were minted at Belgrade until 1640, when almost all mints in the Empire were shut down except those of Constantinople, Baghdad and Cairo. The Belgrade mint was reopened in 1649 only to be shut down for good in 1687, a year before the Austrian invasion. For so long as it worked, it was the most productive of all the mints in the adjacent regions.

The presence of Dubrovnik merchants in Belgrade even before the Ottoman conquest is known from the documents kept by the Archives of Dubrovnik and from many travel accounts, but it is additionally confirmed by the finds of their money that span a good portion of time. In a few larger hoards of silver coins of several European states recovered from the environs of Belgrade, the coinages of Dubrovnik and Venice occur without fail. Gold coins of other European states have also been found, and not in small quantities. Soon after Süleyman I, debasement of the silver akçe resulted in one gold coin being worth 200 and more akçes instead of the previous 50–60. It was a warning that the import into the Ottoman Empire had to be paid in a hard, gold or silver, European currency. The fact should not be overlooked that Ottoman Serbia exported various raw materials and commodities, especially leather, wool and wheat. Much of that traffic was channelled through Belgrade. Thus European currencies, from Venetian, Dutch

(Utrecht) and Austrian to Hungarian and Polish, entered the Ottoman Empire. There soon appeared silver thalers which, after the discovery of America and the arrival of large amounts of silver in Europe, were issued in large quantities by many European states, duchies, cities and rulers. The presence of coinages of European states and cities was reported during the Austro-Turkish wars that began with the Siege of Vienna in 1683. Two episodes of Austrian rule in the eighteenth century, especially the period of mass colonization between 1717 and 1739, brought both large and small copper coins to northern Serbia and Belgrade. In that period the Austrian administration intensified commercial contacts with Central Europe at the expense of merchants from the Adriatic coast. Smaller denominations of Austrian copper circulated in Belgrade even later, under the vassal Principality of Serbia. As a result of border trade, close contacts and the influence of Austrian and Serbian merchants from the neighboring Habsburg Monarchy, they remained in use until the Serbian currency was introduced. The presence in Turkish Belgrade of various currencies, especially lower denominations, required occasional publication of their exchange rates ever since the eighteenth century.

We would like to thank Mr Slobodan Srećković both for generously making his coin collection available for the preparation of this volume and for his years-long fruitful collaboration with the Belgrade City Museum.

SÜLEYMAN I (1520–66) 44
Sultani, gold,
wt 3.45 g, diam. 19 mm
Inv. no 10410

Soon after the conquest in 1521, Belgrade assumed Turkish features and became an important military and trading centre. A Turkish mint, set up in 1562, operated almost interruptedly until 1687. In addition to silver akçes, the Belgrade mint struck gold coins in the name of Süleyman I for a brief four-year period, between 1562 and 1566. They are very rare. One of the six specimens known in the world is shown here. The translation of its Arabic legend reads: *Sultan Süleyman son of Selim Han, may his victory be bright, minted at Belgrade in 926* (year of the Hijra era). The sultan's name and the name of his father, the desire that his victory be bright, as well as the place and date of issue are written in the Arabic script on all Turkish coins.

45 SÜLEYMAN I (1520–66)
Akçe, silver (akçes vary in weight from 0.68 to 0.73 g)
Sl. Srećković Collection

The Belgrade mint, which struck this akçe, was a very productive one. Belgrade was not a frontier town any more. Vast northern territories were now under Ottoman rule, administered by the beylerbeyi (governor-general) of Buda and Timișoara. Süleyman I visited Belgrade twice, as well as the second to him, grand vizier Mehmed Pasha Sokollu, whose building projects in Belgrade have been attested. This akçe has the reverse inscription reading: Minted Belgrade 926 (of the Hijra era).

46 COUNTERFEIT AKÇE
of 1565
Sl. Srećković Collection

This is an old counterfeit, a crime referred to in a firman (the sultan's written order) issued in 1565. Today, a forgery made at the same time as its original is often valued more than the authentic coin. This example bears the mark of the Belgrade mint.

SELIM II (1566–76)
Akçe, struck at the
mint of Srebrenica
Sl. Srećković Collection 47

When Süleyman the Magnificent died at Szigetvar in 1566, Mehmed Sokollu kept his death a secret. He managed to transport the Sultan's body to Belgrade, where it was received by his son, the future Sultan Selim II. It was in Belgrade that Selim II was proclaimed sultan. This akçe was struck in the town of Srebrenica, near the mine of the same name known since Antiquity (Argentariae).

MEHMED III (1595–1603)
Akçe, struck at
the mint of Banjaluka
Sl. Srećković Collection 48

The akçes bearing the mintmark of Banjaluka are very rare. The mint was active at the time the office of beylerbeyi of Rumelia, commander of the European part of the Ottoman Empire, was held by Mustafa, Mehmed Sokollu's son. His seat was at Banjaluka.

49 MUSTAFA I (1617–22)
Onluk (10-akçe coin),
struck at the mint of Belgrade
Sl. Srećković Collection

Besides the akçe, the Empire's smallest but predominant silver, larger denominations were also struck in some periods. The onluk was equal to 10 akçes. According to a well-founded study, the mint of Belgrade produced a total of 500,000 akçes. Unfortunately, not many have survived, because each new sultan had all the akçes issued by his predecessor remelted.

50 MEHMED IV (1648–87)
Para (3-akçe coin),
struck at the mint of Belgrade
Sl. Srećković Collection

The Turkish word para, as a synonym for small change, survived in the name of our national currency. Under the 1873 Law of Silver Coinage of the Principality of Serbia, the dinar, divided into 100 paras, became the monetary unit. The dinar has since been retained as the monetary unit in all state formations deriving their state sovereignty from that of Serbia.

SÜLEYMAN II (1687–91) 51
Mangır, bronze,
struck at the Bosnia mint
Sl. Srećković Collection

This bronze piece bears the name of the Bosnia mint. Belgrade was seized by the Turks in 1521, in the reign of Sultan Süleyman the Magnificent, and thus became a Turkish town. In 1688, under Süleyman II, the Turks lost it to Austria, and it remained in their hands for the next three years.

MAHMUD II (1808–39) 52
New rumi altin, gold,
wt 2.41 g, diam. 2.3 cm
Inv. no 1 (hoard)

In 1980 archaeologists excavated a hoard of 334 Turkish gold coins in the Inner Fortress in Kalemegdan. All were struck in the name of the Sultan Mahmud II. The youngest pieces were issued in the thirteenth year of his reign, which indicates that the hoard was stored after 1821. The obverse bears a tughra surrounded by an Arabic inscription. The reverse informs that the coin was struck at Constantinople in the year 1223 of the Hijra era.

European currencies from the period of Ottoman rule

53 RUDOLF II, Holy Roman emperor (1576–1612) Thaler, silver, wt 28.30 g, diam. 42

The obverse shows the Emperor's bust and a twig below it. Round it runs the inscription RVDOLPHVS·II·D·G·RO·IMS AV·G·H·B·REX. On the reverse is the Habsburg two-headed eagle with a crown above and swords in its claws, as well as the inscription ARCHIDVX·AVS-TRIE * DVX·BVR·MAR·MO·1582. The thaler comes from a hoard discovered in the environs of Belgrade.

54

SIGISMUND BÁTHORY,
Prince of Transylvania
(1581–1602)
Thaler, silver, wt 27.95 g,
diam. 39 mm – Inv. no 104

The obverse shows the ruler holding the sceptre over the shoulder with his right hand and the hilt of his sword with the left. Round his image runs the legend SIGISMVNDVS–BATHORI. The reverse shows the crown and below it a shield supported by two half-naked men. The inscription reads PRINCEPS·TRANSSYLVANIA·1590. The thaler comes from a hoard discovered in the environs of Belgrade.

55 PHILIP III, King of Spain
(1598–1621)
Real, silver, wt 13.30 g,
diam. 32 mm – Inv. no 329

This worn thaler of 1611 is presumed to have reached Belgrade with the army amidst the Austro-Turkish battle for Belgrade late in the seventeenth century. The obverse shows a shield charged with heraldic devices and surmounted by the royal crown. Round it runs the inscription PHILIPHVS·III·D·G. The obverse shield is surrounded with HISPANIARVM REX and the year 1611.

Republic of UTRECHT 56
Ducat, gold, Holland,
wt 3.47 g, diam. 22.5 mm
Inv. no 8968

The coins of Dutch provinces from the time Belgrade was under Turkish rule are often found in the city area. This gold piece was in a hoard of silver and gold coins discovered in Djušina Street in 1988. The obverse shows the standing figure of an armoured knight holding the sword and a handful of arrows, and the year 1639. The surrounding legend reads CONCORDIA·RES–P–AR CRES HOL. The reverse contains a frame inscribed with MO·ORD/PROVIN/FOEDER/BELG·AD/LEG IMP.

57 LEOPOLD I, Holy Roman emperor (1657–1705)
Ducat, Austria, gold, wt 3.42 g, diam. 23 mm – Inv. no 1171

The Turkish campaign against Vienna in 1683 was stopped by the Emperor Leopold. In his reign the Turks were pushed back south across the Sava and Danube rivers. He encouraged the settlement of the recaptured territories by Serbs abandoning Serbia proper. This piece was struck at the mint of Kremnitz in Hungary. The obverse shows the Emperor's standing figure with a sceptre and the globe surmounted by a cross in hands. The mint mark is K–B. The design is surrounded with the legend LEOPOLD·D:G·–·I·S·GH·B·REX. The reverse shows the Virgin holding Christ in her arms and the inscription ·AR·AV·DV·BV·M. (a small shield) ·MO:CO·TV·1678.

MARIA THERESA (1740–80) 58
Kreuzer, Austria, bronze,
wt 11 g, diam. 21 mm
Inv. no 10385

The name of this coin has survived in the Serbian language becoming a synonym for the word money. It is not so often heard nowadays, but an old game is still called "krajcarica" (small kreuzer). This is a 1-kreuzer piece with the obverse showing Maria Theresa's bust surrounded by the inscription M·THERES·DG-RICHE·RA·AVS. On the obverse is a cartouche inscribed with EIN/KREUZER/1762/P.

JOSEPH II, Holy Roman emperor (sole ruler 1780–90) 59
Half-thaler, silver, wt 14.50 g,
diam. 34 mm – Inv. no 10386

The Emperor's unclad bust facing right and the letter A below it (mintmark) are surrounded by the inscription IOSEPH·II·D·G·R·I·S·A·GER·HIE·HVN·BOH·REX. The reverse legend reads ARCH·AVST·DVX·BVRG·LOTH·BRAB·COM·FAN ·1789·

ПЕТАР I. КАРАЂОРЂЕ
SCHWARTZ
10

THE PRINCIPALITY AND KINGDOM OF SERBIA

The restoration of Serbia and its currency 1868–1918

Serbia's struggle for liberation, begun under Karadjordje in 1804 and resumed under Miloš Obrenović in 1815, was crowned with the creation of an independent and internationally recognized state according to a treaty signed at the Congress of Berlin in 1878. The road travelled from the First Serbian Insurrection to the Congress of Berlin was marked by the people's will, effort, sacrifice, valour and by the state-building policy of their leaders of common origin. According to the agreement Prince Miloš reached with the Turks late in 1815 Serbia obtained autonomy under Ottoman suzerainty. The autonomy was expanded at the Conference of Ackermann in 1826, including educational and religious liberties. The Hatt-i sherif of 1830 entitled Serbia to run its internal affairs and Turkish troops withdrew from the Fortress of Belgrade. It was granted unrestricted trade throughout the Ottoman Empire, educational and cultural institutions began to be established, as well as its police forces, health service and, generally, the aspects of social life inspiring the feeling of freedom and independence. The Ottoman feudal system was breaking. Formerly held by Turkish sipahis and now vacant, the plots of arable land in fertile regions such as the Tamnava, Kolubara and Morava valleys were allotted to corporate family groups known as *zadruga*-s, which were to provide the basis for national prosperity. In the 1830s, many Serbs from Bosnia, Herzegovina or the Sandžak settled in Serbia. The composition of town population gradually changed, and within a few decades Serbian merchants and craftsmen became predominant. This overall progress was accompanied by the increasing immigration of former Austrian subjects, settling in Serbia either as public servants or as full-time traders. New crafts were being introduced and a tendency towards factory organization became observable. In the mid-century the foundations were laid of industrial production: canon foundries, candle and soap factories, a textile mill supplying the army, Prince Miloš's brewery, steam-driven mill, brickyard and so forth. The import and export of goods, grains and cattle was balanced. The most prominent place in every respect was occupied by Belgrade, the capital of Serbia since 1841.

It should be borne in mind, however, that Serbia was still under Ottoman suzerainty. It was not entitled to mint its own money although the need was great. In addition to a series of Turkish denominations, there circulated the currencies of 42 different European countries. These included both the gold coinage, held in greater esteem than the Turkish for its fineness, and 23 kinds of silver, dominated by thalers. As all these currencies were "valid", in order to prevent chaos and shear arbitrariness their exchange rates were made public twice a year, on St George and St Demetrius days.

The standard accounting unit was the groš, fictitious money. In calculating payments two kinds of groš were used: the çarşi (market) and the fiscal groš, introduced by Prince

Miloš at the beginning of his reign. The fiscal groš was approximately twice as worth as the market groš, or 1 fiscal = 2 market groš and 8 paras. One fiscal groš was equal to 20 fiscal paras, and 1 market groš to 40 market paras. In payments of the state taxes the calculations were made on the basis of the fiscal groš exchange rate, a rate twice as high as that applied in the market.

This complicated monetary picture, with the presence of a large number of foreign currencies, slowed down trading and produced losses. Tremendous need was felt for a single national currency. Although Serbia had no right to mint its own money, the introduction of a national currency had to be a stage on its way to sovereignty.

Serbia's modern coinage began after the withdrawal of Turkish garrisons in 1867. Although not yet fully independent from Turkey, Serbia expressed such pretensions by minting its own money intended as a symbol of sovereignty. To what extent the project was risky may only be guessed. Prince Mihailo Obrenović had taken all the necessary measures and the first Serbian money was issued in 1869. These were the bronze coins of 1, 5 and 10 (fiscal) paras bearing the portrait of Prince Mihailo and the year 1868. From Vienna, where they had been minted, the coins came to Belgrade in February 1869. The Prince, assassinated in Košutnjak in May 1868, never saw them.

In 1875, under Prince Milan Obrenović, was issued a series of silver coins of 50 paras, 1 and 2 dinars, minted on the standards of the European Latin Union. The name dinar appeared for the first time. It was to become the standard monetary unit of the Kingdom of Serbia and all the subsequent states deriving from Serbia's state sovereignty (except this last, Serbia & Montenegro, the dinar not being a means of payment in Montenegro). In 1876 test prints of the banknotes of 1, 5, 10, 50 and 100 dinars were made but not released.

The first coin series of the Principality of Serbia was issued in 1879. This first series of a now internationally recognized independent state included the copper coins of 5 and 10 paras, the silver coins of 50 paras, 1, 2 and 5 dinars, and the 20-dinar gold coin (also known as Milan d'Or) bearing the Prince's portrait. After it became a kingdom in 1882, a series of 10- and 20-dinar gold coins was issued. When the Bank of Serbia (full name Privileged National Bank of the Kingdom of Serbia) was established and became operative on 2 July 1884, the first Serbian banknote of 100 dinars, redeemable in gold, was issued and dated 2 July. To the pride of Serbia's citizens, it was reliable and much sought-after, and it is recorded that people took gold to the bank in order to exchange it for the paper money.

Despite pressures, such as the Annexation Crisis of 1908 and the destruction and heavy losses suffered during World War One, the Kingdom of Serbia brought into the new state its sound currency whose value had been maintained even amidst the war. The credit rightly goes to Djordje Weiffert, one of the founders of the Bank and its wartime governor. From Marseille, where the Bank had been evacuated, he ensured that the external debt was paid regularly thereby maintaining the credibility of the Serbian dinar.

60 a Copper, wt 1 g,
diam. 15 mm
Inv. no 10388

60 b Copper, wt 5 g,
diam. 15 mm
Inv. no K.26

60 c Copper, wt 10 g,
diam. 30 mm
Inv. no K.2

After the Turks surrendered the Serbian towns in 1867, Prince Mihailo took all the steps required for the introduction and minting of the Serbian coinage. The issue included the coins of 1, 5 and 10 paras (fiscal). Prince Mihailo never had a chance to see them, just as he never set his foot in the National Theatre to the founding and building of which he had contributed so greatly. He had been assassinated in Košutnjak on 29 May 1868. The coins of resurgent Serbia were minted in Vienna after the design of the then famous engravers Anton Scharff and Friedrich Leischek. The effigy of Prince Mihailo dominates the obverse. It is surrounded by the inscription ОБРЕНОВИЋ III. – КЊАЗ СРПСКИ (Obrenović III – Prince of Serbia). The reverse contains the mark of value and the issuing year 1868. On top, between the ends of a wreath is the princely crown.

61 PRINCIPALITY OF SERBIA
1-dinar coin of 1875
Silver, wt 5 g, diam. 23 mm
Inv. no 9393

For the first time in Serbia's modern history, the dinar (equal to 100 paras) became its standard monetary unit under the 1873 Law of Silver Coinage. Two years later, in 1875, the first series of Serbian silver coins in the denominations of 50 paras, 1 and 2 dinars was issued. They were based on the standards of the Latin Monetary Union (fineness, size, weight). Serbia was not a member, but sought to catch up with Europe in that way. It should be remembered that at the time the silver currency was issued Serbia was still under Ottoman suzerainty. Under the abovementioned law, the finance minister was authorized to suppress foreign currencies, and the issuance of the first silver series expressed Serbia's aspirations to independence. This series was also minted in Vienna and designed by the same engravers responsible for the first copper series of 1868. The coin shows the portrait of young Milan Obrenović, his name and title: МИЛАН М. ОБРЕНОВИЋ IV КЊАЗ СРПСКИ. The reverse contains the mark of value and year of issue.

PRINCIPALITY OF SERBIA **62**
5-dinar coin of 1879
Silver, wt 25 g, diam. 37 mm
Inv. no 6820

This five-dinar silver coin belongs to the first issue of the independent Principality of Serbia, internationally recognized as the 25th world's state at the Congress of Berlin in 1878. The issue included the copper coins of 5 and 10 paras, the silver of 50 paras, 1, 2 and 5 dinars, and the gold coin of 20 dinars. They all bear the portrait of Prince Milan Obrenović, the mark of value and year of issue. Despite the fact that the country was exhausted in the wars of liberation waged against Turkey (1876–78), Prince Milan decided to issue larger silver and, for the first time, gold coins. The lettered edge reads: БОГ ЧУВА СРБИЈУ (God guards Serbia).

63 PRINCIPALITY OF SERBIA
10-dinar note of 1876
Test prints of the first notes of the Principality of Serbia
131 × 96 mm
Djordje Novaković Legacy, Inv. no 3

The first Serbian attempt in 1876 at issuing paper currency failed. Only test prints were made (notes of 1, 5, 10, 50 and 100 dinars), 1500 notes for each denomination. After a revolt in Herzegovina in July 1875, Serbia started serious war preparations in spite of an unsympathetic attitude of the Great Powers. Early in 1876, seeking to provide resources for the war effort, it chose to print paper money without gold coverage equal to the planned foreign loan of 24 million dinars. All technical preparations were completed and test prints made at the State Mint in Belgrade. However, the expected loan was not realized and the notes were never put into circulation.

PRINCIPALITY OF SERBIA 20-dinar coins of 1879 and 1882 **64**
Gold coins (Milan d'Or) of the Principality and Kingdom of Serbia
Gold, wt 6.45 g, diam. 21 mm (both issues)

PRINCIPALITY OF SERBIA **64 a**
20 dinars of 1879 – Inv. no 1186

KINGDOM OF SERBIA **64 b**
20 dinars of 1882 – Inv. no 1282

These gold coins with the portrait and name of Prince and King Milan, called Milan d'Or after him, were Serbia's pride. Both pieces were issued by the independent Serbian state, the first by the Principality of Serbia in 1879, the second by the Kingdom in Serbia in 1882. The earlier one, minted in Paris, is inscribed with МИЛАН IV М. ОБРЕНОВИЋ КЊАЗ СРПСКИ (Milan IV M. Obrenović Prince of Serbia), and the engraver's name Tasset below Prince Milan's portrait. Its reverse contains a wreath with the princely crown between its ends. The later gold coin was minted in Vienna and bears the name of the engraver A. Scharff. The obverse portrait of Milan, now a king, is surrounded with the legend МИЛАН I КРАЉ СРПСКИ (Milan I King of Serbia), the reverse showing the royal crown. Along the edge of both coins runs the legend БОГ ЧУВА

65 Die for the counterfeit 1-dinar coin of the KINGDOM OF SERBIA of 1897 - Inv. no 6836

Ever since coinage has begun, attempts have been made at its counterfeiting. Those doing it undermined trust in the state that acted as guarantor of the authenticity of its money. Counterfeiting was therefore severely punished. As a rule, counterfeiting involved the money that was sought-for and had a considerable purchasing power. This artefact is a die for counterfeiting the 1897 silver dinar of the Kingdom of Serbia with the portrait of King Aleksandar Obrenović. The counterfeit was cast from an alloy that only looked like silver. The concurrent attempts at counterfeiting even paper money suggest that the Serbian currency was a valuable one and that the country's economy, based mostly on agricultural production and the diligence of its citizens, was sound and, as such, provided a basis for the further development of society.

KINGDOM OF SERBIA
66
5-dinar coin of 1904
Silver, wt 25 g, diam. 37 mm
Inv. no 90

The 100th anniversary of the First Serbian Insurrection in 1904 was commemorated throughout the kingdom. At squares and other suitable places memorial fountains were set up. Many vanished in time, for political or urban planning reasons, but the pride and memory have not. The National Bank of the Kingdom of Serbia commemorated the anniversary with a series of 5-dinar silver coins with the portraits of Karadjordje and King Petar I Karadjordjević. In that way the memory of a crucial event from the nation's past was given a permanent form. Minted in Vienna, the coins bear the name of the engraver Schwartz. The lettered edge reads БОГ ЧУВА СРБИЈУ (God guards Serbia).

67 KINGDOM OF SERBIA 5-dinar banknote of 1917
124 × 77 mm - DJNL, Inv. no 25

In spite of the war and destruction, Serbia preserved the value of its money. During the war it printed this 5-dinar banknote redeemable in gold. It was designed at the print works of the Bank of France, where it was printed. It remained in circulation all through to 1935.

100
Ж.429
БЕНАЦА
АЛЕКСАНДАР I КРАЉ СРБА, ХРВАТА И СЛОВЕНАЦА
ШТИНА
ГРАДА
ЗУЈЕ
ДГОВА.
ШЋУ ОД
. НОВЦУ.
ИК
ПАРА
10
PARA

THE KINGDOM OF YUGOSLAVIA

1918–1941

On 1 December 1918, the day a new state, founded on the sovereignty of the two kingdoms, Serbia and Montenegro, was proclaimed, several currencies circulated in its territory. The first few years of the existence of the Kingdom of Serbs, Croats and Slovenes, renamed the Kingdom of Yugoslavia in 1929, were spent in putting its monetary affairs in order, which above all required the unification of currencies (Austro-Hungarian, occupational, Allied). The marking and replacement was based on the Serbian dinar, whose value had been maintained during the war so that 87.3 percent of the total money supply in 1918 was covered by gold reserves. The process of demonetization was carefully controlled, each note being overprinted or stamped. There was a fixed sum each person was allowed to replace, and for that reason records were made. An excess over the fixed amount of the largely devalued money was deposited in the state treasury, but not seized from the depositor.

The first money issued by the new state were 1- and ½-dinar banknotes. The face of the one-dinar note was inscribed with the name of the issuing authority – Ministry of Finance of the Kingdom of Serbs, Croats and Slovenes – in three languages and two scripts, Cyrillic and Latin, followed by the figure 1 and the word dinar (again both in Cyrillic and Latin scripts). The back of the note was inscribed in French. Following a decision of the Ministerial Council of the same year, dinar-crown notes were issued so as to replace both the stamped and overprinted Austro-Hungarian banknotes and those of the Privileged National Bank of the Kingdom of Serbia. They bore the mark of value expressed both in dinars and in Austro-Hungarian crowns. This is the unique case that a national currency bears the mark of value expressed in another national currency. The ratio of the dinar and the crown was 1 to 4. Serbia sacrificed its national currency to common interests. The money was produced in Paris, Prague, Zagreb and Novi Sad in denominations ranging from ½ dinar (or 2 crowns) to 1000 dinars (or 4000 crowns). The latter, and the highest, dinar-crown banknote remained longest in use.

The first coins were struck in 1920 (5, 10 and 25 paras). In 1921 appeared the 25-para (or a quarter of a dinar) note. In 1922 and 1923, the 10-, 100- and 1000-dinar notes were released. In 1925 the nickel coins of 50 paras, 1 and 2 dinars were struck, and also the first 20-dinar coin in gold.

Late in 1929 building of the State Mint in Topčider in Belgrade was finished. By the middle of the following year it had been fully operative. The first banknote it produced was the 10-dinar note dated 26 May 1929.

On 1 January 1933 the banknote of 1000 dinars, designed by the painter Paja Jovanović, was issued. It was dated 1 December 1931 and was the first to bear the portrait of a woman, Queen Marija Karadjordjević. Some other banknotes will also be shown in this chapter, including the reserve issue of 1941 many of which were overprinted and thus turned into the so-called Nedić money (1941–44), as well as the last issue prepared by the government-in-exile of the Kingdom of Yugoslavia in 1943 but never issued.

68 1000-dinar/4000-crown note of 1919
Kingdom of Serbs, Croats and Slovenes,
236 × 133 mm – DJNL, Inv. no 220

When the new state was formed, Kingdom of Serbs, Croats and Slovenes, several national currencies were in circulation, most of all those from the former Austro-Hungarian Monarchy. Therefore steps were taken to carry out their unification. Firstly, the money of the former and occupying states was marked. The next step was issuance of banknotes bearing the mark of value expressed both in dinars and in crowns. They were exchanged only for the previously marked money. Their gradual withdrawal was completed in 1934, the last withdrawn being this one.

100-dinar note of 1920
Kingdom of Serbs, Croats and Slovenes,
169 × 100 mm - DJNL, Inv. no 252

69

Preparations for this note, dated 30/11/1920, were long. Printed in France, it was released as late as 1 January 1925. With the issuance of the "blue hundred", as it was popularly known, began the withdrawal of the 1905 series of the same denomination issued by the Kingdom of Serbia and of the 1919 dinar-crown series.

70 10-para note of 1920
Municipality of Belgrade, 80 × 48 mm
DJNL, Inv. no 159

Great destitution and a monetary chaos in the aftermath of World War One generated the need for a stable currency in circulation. The local authorities in several towns and cities of the new state responded timely by issuing their own municipal money. From the information on the notes issued by the Municipality of Belgrade it can be seen that they were convertible into the corresponding amount of the state-issued money at the municipal cashier's.

20-dinar coin of 1925 71
Kingdom of Serbs, Croats and Slovenes,
gold, wt 6.45 g, diam. 21 mm
Inv. no 2189

Several curiosities surround this gold coin. First of all, it was struck in Paris in 1927 but dated 1925. Secondly, although a legal means of payment, it was never put into everyday circulation. It could be bought at the National Bank and only for another country's gold currency. Its principal function was as a deposited security for the state loans and the money in circulation. This function is also indicated by the mintage of one million pieces (6.45 tons of gold).

72 10-dinar note of 1929
Kingdom of Yugoslavia, 126 × 82 mm
DJNL, Inv. no 259

There are two types of this banknote. One was issued in the name of the Kingdom of Serbs, Croats and Slovenes (1926), the other in that of the Kingdom of Yugoslavia (1929). The earlier bears the signature of Governor Djordje Weiffert, the later that of I. J. Bajloni. The 1926 note was printed in Paris; for the 1929 one the modified Paris plates were used and it was the first note produced by the State Mint in Belgrade.

20-dinar coin of 1938 73
Kingdom of Yugoslavia,
silver, wt 9 g, diam. 27 mm
Inv. no 9417

The issuance of this silver coin reflects the position and stability of the Yugoslav currency. The stability of the dinar was obvious until the war broke in 1941, as evidenced by exchange rates. The edge inscription "God guards Yugoslavia" occurs in Latin script (BOG ČUVA JUGOSLAVIJU) on the 20-dinar coin and in Cyrillic script (БОГ ЧУВА JУГОСЛАВИJУ)

74 100-dinar note of 1942
Serbia, 65 × 84 mm
DJNL, Inv. no 739

The money circulating during the German occupation is known as the "Nedić money". After the Kingdom of Yugoslavia was torn apart, the occupying authorities demanded for a government of Serbia to be established. General Milan Nedić took up the unrewarding office of prime minister. The Cabinet was answerable to the German Military Command. The reserve issues of the Kingdom of Yugoslavia deposited at the central bank were overprinted and the money flow restored.

75

1000-dinar note of 1943
Kingdom of Yugoslavia, specimen, 177 × 65 mm
DJNL, Inv. no 765

This is the last note bearing the name of the Kingdom of Yugoslavia. The note with the portrait of King Petar II was printed by the National Bank in exile. It was never released and is an exceptional rarity.

SLOVENIJA
DINARJEV
ФАЛСИФИКОВАЊЕ
СЕ КАЖЊАВА
ПО ЗАКОНУ
ДИНАР
DINAR
1
DINAR·ДИНАР·DINAR
1
1991
T. KRNJA

SOCIALIST YUGOSLAVIAS
1944–1992

A result of different occupying forces was a multitude of currencies in the territory of Yugoslavia in the aftermath of World War Two: Croatian kuna, Nedić dinar, Bulgarian lev, Italian lira, Hungarian pengö, German mark, Albanian franc and lek. That preparations for the unavoidable replacement of all these currencies were well-timed may be seen from the fact that they had started even before the war ended. Namely, during the war bodies of the future state ensured the printing of dinar notes in the USSR in the name of Democratic Federative Yugoslavia. Immediately after the war, the printing plates were brought to Yugoslavia, where printing was resumed. The process of replacement, however, was not at all like the one implemented after World War One. Replacement rates were set, but they had no backing in reality. The owners of occupational currencies were given an equivalent up to 5000 DFY dinars, and were paid the rest subsequently but with a 5–70 % deduction, depending on the sum and the owner's political "qualifications".

For the first time in its long history Belgrade found itself in a republican state. The social, political and economic systems had undergone a drastic change. Monarchy was replaced by republic, a unitary state by a federal, a capitalist economy by a socialist, the factors of production, formerly mostly in private ownership, now became state-owned and, later, socially owned. The state was officially constituted on 30 January 1946 when the Constitution of the Federative People's Republic of Yugoslavia was ratified. On 7 April 1963 it was renamed the Socialist Federative Republic of Yugoslavia (SFRY) and bore that name for the next thirty years.

The national currency value was now set by the state with the approval from the International Monetary Fund. It was expressed in gold, i.e. in US dollars, until 1971, when the fixed price of gold was abandoned. The practice of fixing the exchange rate of the dinar to the price of gold continued until 1973, when the floating exchange rate was adopted. Thenceforward the exchange rate of the dinar has been expressed in relation to one or several convertible currencies. It did not entail the convertibility of the dinar, however, because the different economic and market systems of socialist and capitalist countries did not allow a clear parity between their currencies.

All those numerous adjustments of the dinar in relation to gold or a convertible foreign currency went with a steady descent of its value. The number of zeroes on notes and of notes themselves kept rising. For the first time in its history, the state had to resort to redenomination, and twice: on 1 August 1965, when two zeroes were "wiped off", or 100 old dinars became worth 1 new dinar; and on 1 January 1990 when 10,000 dinars became equal to 1 new dinar. This new dinar was proclaimed convertible but the truth was different. International monetary bodies had never recognized the socialist dinar as a convertible currency. The period immediately preceding the SFRY's bloody break when Western currencies were obtainable at domestic banks, a time that many remember with a sense of longing, was in fact a period of the so-called internal convertibility. It lasted briefly, practically for so long as the foreign exchange reserves permitted it.

Several changes of the state's name, twice redenominated and steadily depreciating dinar gave rise to many different denominations. Between 1944 and 1992 no less than 67 different banknotes, 156 types of coins and 80 types of commemorative coins were issued.

76 1-dinar note of 1944
Design dim. 81 × 39 mm
DJNL, Inv. no 812

An issue of the state named Democratic Federative Yugoslavia, this note had been printed even before the war ended, at first in the USSR, at the Moscow state mint, and after the war in Yugoslavia. Officially issued on 20 April 1945, it remained a means of payment until 1956. It was designed by Djordje Andrejević-Kun, with the war veteran Milivoj Radić posing for the portrait of a partisan soldier. The series included eight denominations: 1, 5, 10, 20, 50, 100, 500 and 1000 dinars. All of them bore the same design differing only in colour and size.

100-dinar note of 1946 | 77
Design dim. 121 × 56 mm
DJNL, Inv. no 998

This note belongs to the first postwar series issued by the National Bank of the newly-formed state (FNRJ/FPRY), which also included the 50-, 500- and 1000-dinar notes. The issuing date is 1 May 1946, the first postwar Labour Day. The practice of issuing new series dated 1 May was continued in the following decades. The face and back show the fisherman, the blacksmith and the reaper, as symbols of the fast pace at which the country was recovering after the war.

78 100-dinar note of 1963
127 × 60 mm
DJNL, Inv. no 1029

In the mid-1950s, after a turn in the country's foreign policy, different designs began to be introduced. In this note, considered by many as the most beautiful ever issued by socialist Yugoslavia, motifs of postwar reconstruction were replaced by softer scenes. The face bears the smiling image of a girl from Konavli dressed in the local costume, while the back, in full colour, shows a view of Dubrovnik. The red colour has ever since been characteristic of the notes of 10, 100, 1000, 10,000 and even one million dinars.

79 5000-dinar note of 1985
164.5 × 75 mm

This note marked the beginning of a trend of redesigning paper money. The design of paper money followed the newly established pattern not only in the SFRY but throughout the inflationary 1990s. It was the first time that a note of socialist Yugoslavia showed the effigy of an historical figure. The portrait of Josip Broz Tito, lifelong president of Yugoslavia, appeared on this note five years after his death. The issuance of notes bearing his portrait may have been the last attempt to uphold his personality cult, a symbol of the state whose break was on the horizon.

80 1 dinar of 1991
Wt 5.95 g,
diam. 24 mm

This is the last 1-dinar coin struck by the SFRY on the eve of its break. Virtually throughout the period this chapter deals with the coinage of lower denominations followed a more or less uniform pattern. The reverses generally bear only the mark of value and the obverses the national arms.

РОДНА БАНКА ЈУГОСЛАВИЈЕ
ARODNA BANKA JUGOSLAVIJE
ДИНАРА·DINARA
20
НАРОДНА БАНКА
ЈУГОСЛАВИЈЕ
1000
000

HYPERINFLATION AND LAST YUGOSLAVIA

When the Federal Republic of Yugoslavia, the so-called third Yugoslavia, was constituted on 27 April 1992 the fragmentation of the SFR Yugoslavia was almost completed. Fierce wars accompanying the secession of one SFRY republic after another were still going on and were to be fought for another few years. In the new state remained Serbia and Montenegro. The loss of former Yugoslavia's big market was aggravated by the country's total economic isolation caused by UN sanctions. Under such circumstances, a decrease in industrial production, shortages of goods, a rise of prices, hyperinflation and a decreasing standard of living were unavoidable.

Soon after the new state was constituted, new notes were printed. Inflation already being at an upsetting level, redenomination was carried out on 1 July 1992, only a year and a half after the previous one. This time only one zero was looped off so that 10 SFRY dinars were replaced by 1 SRY dinar. The next redenomination came even sooner and on 1 October 1993 six zeroes were wiped off so that one new dinar was nominally worth one million old dinars. The last redenomination in this hyperinflationary period took place on 1 January 1994 at a rate of one billion dinars to one dinar. The overall descent of the dinar's face value in the FRY alone was 10 thousand trillion times (10,000,000 ,000,000,000), and with two redenominations under the SFRY added even ten billion trillion times (10,000,000,000, 000,000,000,000). A total of 22 zeroes were removed.

The rate of inflation was beyond the grasp of the ordinary man. Changes in the exchange rate in relation to the deutschmark, the black market's preferred currency, became a matter of hours. Towards the end of the hyperinflation period the dinar virtually ceased to exist as a means of payment. Most sellers of any kind of goods were only willing to accept hard currencies. Paper and metal money of all West European countries was in circulation.

If this monetary situation is seen through the same factors as the periods presented previously – money as a symbol and reality of the sovereignty of a state, or the pre-eminence of a ruler's currency in his realm – a striking inference may be drawn. The paper money issued in those years bore neither the full name nor the arms of the issuing state, while foreign currencies took precedence. From the perspective of the money in circulation, therefore, Serbia of the period may be interpreted as a European dependency.

In January 1994 the monthly rate of hyperinflation reached 314 million percent. The situation was critical and on 24 January 1994 the Programme for the Monetary Reconstruction and Economic Recovery of Yugoslavia was adopted. A new currency was introduced as a means of payment – the new dinar. Its value was pegged to the deutschmark at a rate of 1 to 1, and replacement of the old money with the new began at the rate of 1 new dinar to 13 million old dinars.

The period of galloping hyperinflation was thus brought to an end. From the perspective of notaphily and numismatics this process of devaluation is exceptionally interesting. In no more than 21 months (1992–94) 33 new kinds of notes and 12 coin types were issued. On the paper money 12 figures from national history were shown, the portrait of Nikola Tesla being used five times.

The abovementioned monetary reform stabilized to an extent the exchange rate as compared with the previous period and, accordingly, the number of new notes was reduced. The new banknotes finally came to bear the name (FR Yugoslavia) and arms of the issuing state. The arms were placed on coins only in 1996.

Changes following the election of September 2000 reflected in money as well. No later than mid-December the same year the new government issued the first series of coins (50 paras, 1, 2, and 5 dinars) and notes (20, 50 and 100 dinars). Our currency was given back its old name, dinar instead of new dinar. In order to facilitate circulation, but also as a result of inflation, the denominations of 10, 200, 1000 and 5000 dinars have been subsequently introduced.

The latest change in the structure and name of the state took place on 4 February 2003 with the adoption of the Constitutional Charter of Serbia and Montenegro. It found expression in money, but our local developments have once more established a precedent in the international monetary practice. Although we are living in a state union named Serbia and Montenegro, Serbia's currency is issued by the National Bank of Serbia and does not function as a means of payment in the other member state. Once again, this shows to what extent all changes that a state undergoes can be read from the money in circulation; even if the official information communicates a different message. Messages that have been conveyed by money since Antiquity seem to contain important and illuminating information about the issuing authority, its strength and objectives.

500-billion-dinar note of 1993
151 × 72 mm
81

This denomination with, face, the portrait of Jovan Jovanović Zmaj and, back, the building of the National Library of Serbia, holds the infamous record for the number of zeroes. Issued on 23 December 1993, this note has remained the symbol of one of the highest ever registered inflation rates in the world. A redenomination that followed only seven days later rendered it unusable.

82 1 para of 1994
Wt 2.718 g, diam. 17 mm
Inv. no 9521

After the dinar was stabilized and virtually a new currency introduced – the new dinar, the need arose for lower coin denominations. After 1868, when Serbian coinage was restored by the Principality of Serbia and the 1-para coin with the portrait of Mihailo Obrenović struck, it was only in 1994 that this denomination appeared for the second time in the history of our currency.

1000-dinar note of 2001
151 × 72 mm

83

The face of this note bears the portrait of Djordje Weiffert and a view of his one-time brewery. The back shows Weiffert in his years-long office of governor – the interior of the National Bank of Serbia. Such a scene seems to have aimed at evoking the potentials of enterprise, private ownership and a stable dinar the government sought to revive at the time this banknote was issued.

84 20-dinar coin of 2003
Wt 9 g, diam. 28 mm

The new coin series issued late in 2000 broke with the traditions of socialist Yugoslavias. For the first time since World War One an artistic representation has appeared on coinage. The latest series issued by the National Bank of Serbia shows the Bank building, the monasteries of Gračanica, Krušedol, Studenica and the Church of St Sava (denominations of 1, 2, 5, 10 and 20 dinars respectively). These are the first Serbia's coins in 87 years.

BIBLIOGRAPHY

* In this bibliography the titles of the works published in Serbian are quoted in the language in which their summaries, or integral texts in case of bilingual publication, have been published.

The title of the annual published by the Belgrade City Museum occurs both in French and in English. Namely, until 1997 and its 44th issue the title-page was given in French (*Annuaire de la ville de Belgrade*) and since that year in English (*Annual of the City of Belgrade*).

Basic bibliography

Sylloge Nummorum Graecorum, The Royal Collection of Coins and Medals, Danish National Museum, Copenhagen 1943

Popović P., *Les monnayage des Scordisques* Beograd – Novi Sad 1987

Roman Imperial Coinage I-X, London 1923

Wroth W *Imperial Byzantine Coins*, Chicago 1966

Huszár L., *Münzkatalog Ungarn: von 1000 bis heute*, München–Battenberg 1979

Ivanišević V, *Serbian Medieval Coinage*, Belgrade 2001

Mihailović V, *The Coinage of the Serbian Regional Lords During the Empire*, Belgrade 2000

Jovanović M., *Serbian Medieval Coins*, Belgrade 2002

Nuri Pere, *Osmanlilarda madeni paralar*, Istanbul 1968

Srećković S., *Akches* I-III, Belgrade 1999-2003

Srećković S., *Ottoman Mints & Coins*, Belgrade 2002

Kabaklarli N., *Mangir*, Istanbul 1998

Papadopuli N., *Le Monete di Venezia*, I – Venezia 1893; II – Venezia 1907; III – Milano 1919; III/2 – Milano 1919

Vinaver V., *Pregled istorije novca u jugoslovenskim zemljama (XVI-XIX vek)*, Beograd 1970

Hadži-Pešić J., *Novac Srbije* 1868-1918, Beograd 1995

Hadži-Pešić J., *Novac Kraljevine Jugoslavije 1918-1941*, Beograd 1995

Hadži-Pešić J., *Novac Jugoslavije 1944-1992*, Beograd 1995

Hadži-Pešić J., *Novac Jugoslavije 1992-1996*, Beograd 1999

Numismatic studies of the Belgrade area

Borić-Brešković B., *Coins of Viminacium in the Collection of Svetozar St. Dušanić*, Belgrade City Museum, Collections and Legacies VII, Belgrade 1976

Birtašević M., Restes en argent de bijoux et de monnaies du village de Ritopek, *Annual of the City of Belgrade* IV, Belgrade 1957, 53-59

Валтровић М., Босански новци нађени у атару села Лисог Поља, *Старинар* 1, Београд 1884, 32-41

Vasić M.R., Le dépôt des pièces d'or romain de Belgrade, *Annual of the City of Belgrade* XV, Belgrade 1968, 237-245

Г(авриловић) І(ован), Налазакъ римски древны новаца у Београду, *Новине Сербске*, бр. 21, додатак, Београд 1840, 116

Elmer G., Ein Fund römischen Goldmünzen aus Borča, *Numismatische Yeitschrift* 23, Wien 1930, 39-46

Ivanišević V., Hinterlassenschaft türkischen Herrschaft bis zu dem Winerkrieg *Annual of the City of Belgrade* XXX, Belgrade 1983, 27-39

Ivanišević V., Two Findings of IV Century Bronze Coins from the Belgrade Fortress, *Numizmatičar* 6, Belgrade 1983, 77-97

Ivanišević V., The Finding of Roman Bronze Coins from the Years 375-8 A.D. from the Belgrade Fortress, *Numizmatičar* 9, Belgrade 1986, 44-59

Ivanišević V., Byzantine Coins from the Belgrade Fortress, *Numizmatičar* 10, Belgrade 1987, 88-110

Ivanišević V., A Hoard of Gold Coins from European Countries of 17th Century Found in the Belgrade Fortress, *Annual of the City of Belgrade* XXXVI, Belgrade 1989, 93-99

Kondić V., *Monnaie à Belgrade*, Musée de la ville de Beograd, Catalogues des expositions 6, Beograd 1967

Kondić V., Une trouvaille de monnaies en or romaines à Ušće près d'Obrenovac, *Starinar XVIII*, Beograd 1968, 207-213

Kondić V., *The Singidunum hoard of denarii and antoniniani*, Monographs, The Belgrade City Museum, Beograd 1969

Ljubić Š., Skrovište rimskih carskih novaca u zlatu iz prvog stoleća odkrito u Zemunu 16. prosinca 1875, *Rad Jugoslovenske akademije znanosti i umetnosti* XXXVI, Zagreb 1876, 177-200

Ljubić Š., Odkriće ugarskih novaca u Boljevcih kod Zemuna, *Viestnik Hrvatskoga arkeologičkoga družtva* 1, Zagreb 1879, 27-28

Mattson G.O., A Hoard of Turkish Akches found in Belgrade, *Numismatic Chronicle* 19, London 1955, 165-174

Mihailović V., A Hoard of Roman Aes (Avgvstvs - Nero) from the Mining Districts of Kosmaj, *Numizmatičar* 17, 25-34

Novaković S., Serbian Medieval Coins in the Belgrade City Museum, *Annual of the City of Belgrade XXXIII*, Belgrade 1986, 25-37

Novaković S., Serbian Medieval Coins in the Cabinet for Coins and Medals in the Belgrade City Museum, *Annual of the City of Belgrade* XXXVII, Belgrade 1990, 85-89

Petrović J., Ein grosser fund griechischer drachmen aus Zaklopača, *Starinar* VII, Beograd 1932, 40-65

Srećković S., The First Minting of Coins in Belgrade, *Annual of the City of Belgrade* XXXV, Belgrade 1988, 61-73

Tapavički M., New finds of Roman coins from Kosančićev Venac No. 12-16 in Belgrade, *Numizmatičar* 21, Belgrade 1998, 54-62

Crnobrnja N.A., The List and Map of the Finds of Antique Coins in the Territory of Belgrade, *Annual of the City of Belgrade* XXV, Belgrade 1978, 197-211

Crnobrnja N.A., The Roman Republican Denarii from the Cabinet for Coins and Medals in the Museum of the City of Belgrade, *Annual of the City of Belgrade* XXVI, Belgrade 1979, 5-15

Crnobrnja N.A., Le dépôt de la monnaie romaine de Belgrade exemplaires de nouvelles émissions de Constance II, Constance Gallus et Jules César, *Annual of the City of Belgrade* XXVII, Belgrade 1980, 23-33

Crnobrnja N.A., Types of Scordiscian minimi in the collection of The Museum of the City of Belgrade, *Archaeologia Yugoslavica* XX-XXI, Beograd 1980-1981

Crnobrnja N.A., Coins of the Town of Nicaea in the Numismatic Collection of the Museum of the City of Belgrade, *Annual of the City of Belgrade* XXVIII, Belgrade 1981, 23-27

Crnobrnja N.A., Celtic Coins in the Cabinet for Coins and Medals of the City Museum of Belgrade, *Annual of the City of Belgrade* XXIX, Belgrade 1982, 5-13

Crnobrnja N.A., An Antoninianus of Philip II as sole Emperor, *Numizmatičar* 7, Belgrade 1987, 137-142

Crnobrnja N.A., *Coins from the Area of Zemun up to 1521*, Belgrade City Museum, Collections and Donations Catalogue XVI, Belgrade 1984

Crnobrnja N.A., The Ancient Coins Found at Ušće near Obrenovac, *Annual of the City of Belgrade* XXXII, Belgrade 1985, 51-79

Crnobrnja N.A., Antique coins from the area of Roman road Singidunum-Castra Tricornia-Ad Sextum miliarem belonging to the Numismatics collection of the Museum of the City of Belgrade, *Annual of the City of Belgrade* XXXIII, Belgrade 1987, 29-65

Crnobrnja N.A., The Find of Bronze Roman Coins from Batajnica, *Numizmatičar* 11, Belgrade 1998, 55-58

Crnobrnja N.A., Of Aurei-Minimi Scordisci from the Collection of Velimir Čeleketić, *The Journal of the Serbian Archaeological Society* 5, Belgrade 1989, 151-154

Crnobrnja N.A., A Find of Coins from European Countries of 17th Century Excavated in Studentski Park in Belgrade, *Annual of the City of Belgrade* XXXVI, Belgrade 1989, 85-93

Crnobrnja N.A., Scordiscian Coins – Donation of the Beogradska Banka D.D., *Annual of the City of Belgrade* XXXVII, Belgrade 1990, 29-39

Crnobrnja N.A., Three Hoards of Roman Bronze Coins (IV Century) from the Area of the Municipality of Obrenovac, *Numizmatičar* 14, Belgrade 1991, 41-48

Crnobrnja N.A., Surveying of the Obrenovac Municipality Area, *The Journal of the Serbian Archaeological Society* 8, Belgrade 1992, 152-158

Crnobrnja N.A., *The Coins of the Province of Dacia in the Collection of Svetozar St. Dušanić*, Belgrade City Museum, Collections and Donations Catalogue 24, Belgrade 1993

Crnobrnja N.A., The Roman Deposit from Dobanovci (3rd Century), *The Journal of the Serbian Archaeological Society* 9, Belgrade 163-172

Crnobrnja N.A., The Inscription of a Cross on a Antoninian of the Empress Salonina, *Numizmatičar* 17, Belgrade 1994, 35-46

Crnobrnja N.A., Roman coins from Klisina and Pustara in Batajnica, *The Journal of the Serbian Archaeological Society* 10, Belgrade 1995, 128-138

Crnobrnja N.A. – **Čeleketić V.**, Finds of Antique Money on the Localities Klisina and Pustara in Batajnica – Part II, *The Journal of the Serbian Archaeological Society* 12, Belgrade 1996, 179-190

Crnobrnja N.A., Roman Coins from the "Kaludjerske Livade" at Surčin, *Annual of the City of Belgrade* XLIII, Belgrade 1996, 33-37

Crnobrnja N.A., A Group find of antique coins from Ugrinovci, *Annual of the City of Belgrade* XLIV, Belgrade 1997, 5-11

Crnobrnja N.A., Roman Coinage from the 1st to the 6th Century, in *Antique Bronze from Singidunum*, Belgrade City Museum, Catalogues of exhibitions 49, Belgrade 1997, 341-383

Crnobrnja N.A. – Čeleketić V., Finds of Antique Money on the Localities Klisina and Pustara in Batajnica (3rd part), *The Journal of the Serbian Archaeological Society* 14, Belgrade 1998, 233-240

Crnobrnja N.A. and **Ujes D.**, Greek Coins in the Numismatic Collection of the City Museum of Belgrade, *The Journal of the Serbian Archaeological Society* 15-16, Belgrade 1999-2000, 185-209

Crnobrnja N.A., Hrišćanski tragovi na novcu cara Galijena i carice Salonine kao odraz edikta o verskom miru 261. godine i prvom javnom uvažavanju Hrišćanske Crkve, *Glasnik Srpske pravoslavne Crkve,* godina LXXXIII, br. 4, Beograd 2001, 82-88

Crnobrnja A.N., Govor novca, *Republika* 279, Beograd 2002, 14-16

Šipuš N., Roman Coins Found at the Village of Ušće near Obrenovac, *Annual of the City of Belgrade* XXXIII, Belgrade 1986, 5-25

TABLE OF CONTENTS

МУЗЕЈ ГРАДА БЕОГРАДА
BELGRADE CITY MUSEUM

www.mgb.org.yu

CIP – Каталогизација у публикацији
Народна библиотека Србије, Београд

069.51:737.1 (497.11) (083.824)
737.1 (083.824)
336.746/ .747 (497.1) (083.824)

CRNOBRNJA, ADAM
Belgrade's History From the Numismatic Record / by Adam Crnobrnja, Nikola Crnobrnja; [translation Marina Adamović-Kulenović; photographs by Nebojša Borić, Vladimir Popović]. – Beograd : Belgrade City Museum = Музеј града Београда, 2004 (Beograd : Alexandria studio). - 152 str. : ilustr. ; 24 cm. - (Monographies / Belgrade City Museum ; 11)

Izv. stv. nasl.: Новац у Београду кроз векове. - Tiraž 1.200. – Str. 3-4: Preface to the English edition / Bojan Kovačević. – Bibliografija: str. 141-148.

ISBN 86-80619-29-9

a) Muzej grada Beograda. Kabinet za novac i medalje - Izložbeni katalozi b) Novac – Beograd - Izložbeni katalozi
COBISS.SR-ID 119432460